BPI YEARBOOK 2012

Recorded Music in the UK: Facts, Figures and Analysis

© 2012 BPI Limited

No part of this book may be reproduced in any form without written permission from the copyright owner.

ISBN 978-0-906154-33-5

ISSN 0142-7636

May 2012

Designed by Sherry

Edited by Christopher Green
Compiled by Robin Crutchley

The BPI gratefully acknowledges the assistance provided by organisations which have supplied data for this yearbook. All original data sources are quoted throughout. Thanks are also due to Rhona Levene and Marnie Lodhi for their contribution to picture research, Eamonn Forde for his work on the digital chapter and to those organisations and individuals who have provided illustrations. A list of photo credits appears on page 94.

Tables sourced 'Official Charts Company' and 'Millward Brown' contain data derived from the chart compilation exercise over a period of years and BPI extends its thanks to The Official Charts Company for co-operation in the publication of data covering the period 1994-2011.

BPI is a joint venture partner in The Official Charts Company for the publication and exploitation of charts data.

The editor's thanks go to Peter Scaping for his assistance in producing this yearbook.

BPI Limited
Riverside Building
County Hall
Westminster Bridge Road
London SE1 7JA

Telephone: 020 7803 1300
Fax: 020 7803 1310
www.bpi.co.uk

The Official Charts Company
Riverside Building
County Hall
Westminster Bridge Road
London SE1 7JA

Telephone: 020 7620 7450
www.theofficialcharts.com

Contents

Introduction and Annual Review	6
Industry Income	8
Breakdown of Record Company Revenues (2008-2011)	8
Digital's Share of Industry Revenues (2004-2011)	8
Industry Income (2002-2011)	9
Retail Sales	10
Retail Sales by Format – Albums (2005-2011)	10
Format Split (2005-2011)	10
Retail Sales by Format – Singles (2005-2011)	11
Format Split (2005-2011)	11
Best Sellers	12
Top 20 Best Selling Albums (2011)	12
Top 20 Best Selling Singles (2011)	13
Nationality	14
UK Album Sales by Country of Artist's Origin (2007-2011)	14
UK Singles Sales by Country of Artist's Origin (2007-2011)	15
Sales by Type of Music	16
Album Sales by Genre (2002-2011)	16
Singles Sales by Genre (2002-2011)	17
Pop Album Sales by Sub-Genre (2009-2011)	18
Pop Artist/Compilation Sales Split (2011)	18
Pop Digital/Physical Split (2011)	18
Top 10 Best Sellers – Pop (2011)	19
Profile: Ed Sheeran's +	19
Top 10 Best Sellers – Rock (2011)	20
Rock Album Sales by Sub-Genre (2009-2011)	20
Rock Artist/Compilation Sales Split (2011)	20
Rock Digital/Physical Split (2011)	20
Top 10 Rock Best Sellers – Vinyl (2011)	21
Urban Artist/Compilation Sales Split (2011)	22
Urban Digital/Physical Split (2011)	22
Profile: Chase and Status's No More Idols	23
Top 10 Best Sellers – Urban (2011)	23
Profile: David Guetta's Nothing But The Beat	24
Top Five Best Sellers – Dance (2011)	24
Dance Artist/Compilation Sales Split (2011)	24
Dance Digital/Physical Split (2011)	24
Profile: Alfie Boe's Bring Him Home and Alfie	25
Top Five Best Sellers – MOR/Easy (2011)	25
MOR/Easy Artist/Compilation Sales Split (2011)	25
MOR/Easy Digital/Physical Split (2011)	25
Classical	26
Profile: Hyperion	26
Classical Sales and Market Share (2004-2011)	26
Classical Artist/Compilation Sales Split (2011)	26
Classical Digital/Physical Split (2011)	26
Top 10 Classical Albums (2011)	27
Classical Market Share by Record Company (2006-2011)	27
Sales Metrics	28
Average Weekly Album Sales by Chart Position (2002-2011)	28
Top Sellers as a Percentage of Total Albums Market (2006-2011)	28
Average Weekly Singles Sales by Chart Position (2002-2011)	29
Top Sellers as a Percentage of Total Singles Market (2006-2011)	29
Number of Albums Sold by Sales Threshold (2002-2011)	30
Number of Singles Sold by Sales Threshold (2002-2011)	31
Monthly Sales Patterns – Albums (2004-2011)	32
Album Sales by Day of Week (2007-2011)	32
Monthly Sales Patterns – Singles (2004-2011)	33
Singles Sales by Day of Week (2007-2011)	33
Regional Sales by Genre and Format (2011)	34
Physical Format Sales – Split by Variant (2011)	35
Vinyl Sales – Split by Variant (2011)	35
Music Gifting – Penetration (2009-2011)	36
Music Gifting – Expenditure by Age (2009-2011)	36
Music Gifting – Expenditure by Gender and Social Group (2009-2011)	36
Reason for Purchase – Artist vs Compilations (2011)	37
Reason for Purchase – Physical Albums (2011)	37
Purchase Type by Buyer Group (2011)	37
Pricing	38
Average Retail Prices – Albums (2009-2011)	38
CD Albums – Sales by Price Group (2009-2011)	38
Average Prices Paid for CD Albums by Retailer Type (2009-2011)	38
Albums Sales by Price Category (2008-2011)	39
Mid-Price Top Sellers (2011)	39
Budget Top Sellers (2011)	39
New Releases and Catalogue	40
Profile: The Vaccines' Whatever Happed To The Vaccines	40
Number of Breakthrough Artists (2007-2011)	40
Number of Debut Breakthrough Albums (2007-2011)	40
Highest Week One Sales – Albums (2011)	41
Biggest Selling Debut Albums (2011)	41
Profile: Why Pink Floyd? campaign	42
Top 10 Back Catalogue Albums (2011)	42
Back Catalogue Sales – Albums (2011)	42
Top 10 Back Catalogue Singles (2011)	43
Back Catalogue Sales – Singles (2011)	43

Section	Page
Compilations	**44**
Compilation Sales (2004-2011)	44
Average Retail Price of Compilations (2009-2011)	44
Artist/Compilation Album Buyer Overlap (2009-2011)	44
Digital's Share of Compilation Sales (2006-2011)	44
Compilation and Artist Album Sales by Price Category (2009-2011)	45
Compilation and Artist Album Sales Growth by Month (2011)	45
Profile: Clubland	46
Top 20 Best Selling Compilation Albums (2011)	46
Compilation Sales by Type of Retailer (2005-2011)	47
Compilation Sales by Type of Music (2005-2011)	47
Music Video	**48**
Music Video Sales	48
Music Video Sales by Type of Retailer (2007-2011)	48
Top 10 Best Selling Music Videos (2011)	48
Video Sales by Genre (2007-2011)	49
Music Video Market Share by Company (2006-2011)	49
Independent Music	**50**
Top 20 Independent Albums (2011)	50
Independent Companies' Market Share (2004-2011)	50
Independent Market Share by Sector (2011)	51
Profile: Select/Naxos	51
Indpendent Albums – Sales Split by Genre (2011)	52
Independent Albums – Sales Share within Genre (2011)	52
Market Share	**53**
Distributor Market Share – Physical Albums (2005-2011)	53
Record Company Market Share – Albums (2005-2011)	54
Record Company Market Share – Singles (2005-2011)	55
The Year in Digital	**56**
Music Retail	**66**
Value of Retail Sales (2005-2011)	66
Leisure Spending (2011)	66
Key Permanent Music Retail Outlets (2009-2011)	67
Other Music Outlets (2011)	67
Retailer Market Shares – Total Music (2010-2011)	68
Retailer Expenditure by Gender and Age – Total Music (2011)	69
Retailer Expenditure by Lifestage Group – Total Music (2011)	70
Retailer Consumer Profile – Total Music (2011)	71
Retailer Share – Artist and Compilation Albums (2011)	72
Retailers' Genre Profile (2011)	73
Consumer Data	**74**
Retailer Loyalty (2009-2011)	74
Impulse/Planned Purchasing Split (2011)	75
Impulse Purchasers – Demographics (2011)	75
Music Spend by Demographic Group (2011)	76
Music Spend by Lifestage Group (2011)	77
Female Expenditure by Age and Social Group (2011)	78
Male Expenditure by Age and Social Group (2011)	78
Penetration and Average Spend per Buyer (2009-2011)	79
Penetration by Gender, Age and Social Group – Total Music (2009-2011)	80
Penetration by Gender, Age and Social Group – Digital Music (2009-2011)	80
Average Spend per Buyer within Gender, Age and Social Group – Total Music (2009-2011)	81
Average Spend by per Buyer within Gender, Age and Social Group – Digital Music (2009-2011)	81
Crossover of Music Buyers (2010-2011)	82
Importance of Crossover Buyers (2011)	82
Crossover of Music Buyers – Age and Gender Breakdown (2011)	83
Average Spend per Buyer (2011)	83
Spend by Buyer Decile (2011)	84
Spend Composition by Gender, Age and Social Group (2011)	84
'21' Buyers by Consumption Category (2011)	85
Demographic Profile of '21' Buyers	85
Music Consumption	**86**
Key Metrics (2010-2011)	86
Music Services – Monthly Activity (2011)	87
Pirate Sites and Applications – Unique Users per Month (2011)	87
World Market	**88**
Top 10 International Markets (2011)	88
Worldwide Recorded Music Trade Revenues (2010-2011)	88
Breakdown of World Sales (2011)	88
Digital's Share of Industry Revenue by Country (2011)	89
Digital's Share of Global Industry Revenue (2006-2011)	89
Best Selling Albums by British Artists Worldwide (2011)	90
Top 10 Markets by Revenue per Capita (2011)	90
British Artists' Chart Achievements – Germany and France (2009-2011)	91
UK Artists' Share of Album Sales in Germany and France (2006-2011)	91
UK Artists' Share of Album Sales in USA and Canada (2006-2011)	92
UK Artists Selling 1m+ Tracks in USA (2011)	92
Top 10 Albums by British Artists in USA (2011)	93
Top 10 Albums by British Artists in Canada (2011)	93
Picture Credits	**94**

Introduction and Annual Review

If there was a moment that defined music in 2011, it must have been Adele's breathtaking rendition of *Someone Like You* at the BRIT Awards. The performance went on to sell over 230,000 copies, raising substantial funds for our charity the BRIT Trust, and pushed the single to no.1 in the charts for five weeks. But its long-term effect on Adele's career and the UK market was even more significant. Although she was already a significant UK star – Adele's first album *19* went to the top of the charts in its week of release in 2008 – the BRITS performance catapulted her to superstardom, and set her on course to achieve the biggest one-year global album sales total in a decade. One in seven UK households bought a copy of *21* in 2011, which by March of this year has become the sixth-biggest selling album of all time. The international statistics are no less impressive, with 20m global sales reached by April of this year including 6m in America.

At a time when overall sales have continued to struggle, major successes such as these are undeniably heartening. They show that music still matters to people and that artists can still connect with music fans on a grand scale. They also remind us that we have a tremendous well of natural talent here in the UK, supported by labels with the skills and the ambition to break artists internationally.

Indeed, the strength of UK domestic repertoire was one of the features of 2011. Not only did British artists claim the majority share in the UK albums market – artists such as Ed Sheeran, Jessie J and Coldplay cumulatively accounted for 52.7% of sales, their biggest slice 1997 – but new inroads were being made abroad as well. The US in particular has experienced something of a new British invasion, with an all-British top three (Adele, Marsha Ambrosius and Mumford & Sons) in their albums chart in March for the first time in 25 years and hit albums later in the year for Jessie J and Florence & The Machine. Tinie Tempah became the first UK rapper to sell 1m copies with a debut single and the US success has continued into 2012 with The Wanted claiming a top five single and One Direction entering at the top of the Billboard 200 with their debut album, the first UK band ever to do so.

New BPI research has shown the Britain's share of world sales of recorded music climbed to 12.6% overall, performing particularly strongly in the United States (11.7%), Canada (16.2%), France (17%) and Australia (22.5%). It's worth putting this in context: our global share of trade in music is four times the UK's average share of sales of goods and double the UK's average share of trade in services. We can feel justly proud of that achievement and UK consumers would agree – over three quarters of respondents in a 2011 Ipsos MORI/BPI survey agreed that not only were British music's achievements something to be proud of, but that our artists' music helps the reputation of Britain overseas.

Yet this creative and international success did not translate into growth. Despite the release of the biggest selling album of the 21st century, album sales in 2011 fell by 5.6% and trade revenue by 3.4%. Revenues from sales have now fallen by 35% since 2004.

The Government's focus is on economic growth and job creation, and BPI has been pressing Government hard for several years to understand that the difference between growth and decline in the music sector is taking meaningful action to tackle endemic illegal downloading.

The encouraging news is that Government continues to support such action and DCMS in particular has helped to raise the profile of the need for action to deprive pirate sites of funding, by means of more responsible practices on the part of search engines, payment processors and internet advertisers.

But the pace of progress has been dispiritingly slow. On 8th April, the Digital Economy Act passed its second anniversary with the Initial Obligations Code still not published. Best estimates now are that notifications to illegal filesharers will not start going out until 2014 at the earliest, four years after the Act was passed. While the failed judicial review application by BT and Talk Talk partly explains the delay, the apparent lack of urgency on the part of UK Government contrasts poorly with the progress made in France, where HADOPI is already generating positive results, and the United States where a new "copyright alerts" system agreed with broadband companies will be up and running by the end of this year.

We also await with interest the delayed publication of the Green Paper on the Communications Act, to see whether Government will put significant pressure on internet intermediaries, such as search engines and internet advertisers, to implement codes of practice that will ensure they do not support major pirate sites.

Naturally we are doing everything we can to help ourselves. British labels have licensed more digital services than any other country in the world, allowing music fans to choose how they want to access their music legally online, even for free on advertising-supported services. And we have continued to press forward with the Music Matters campaign, reminding people of the enduring value of music.

In terms of direct action against piracy, we increased the number of illegal files taken down off the internet by BPI to more than 4 million in 2011, and we obtained a judgment finding that The Pirate Bay infringes the rights of BPI and PPL members in the UK. The second stage of this case, applications to block the site via UK ISPs, is due to be decided shortly. Yet while progress in this case is encouraging for the future, the cost and length of time needed to bring such legal proceedings amply demonstrates the need for an expedited procedure to block major illegal sites.

Government has made no progress on this issue since deciding last year not to implement the relevant sections of the Digital Economy Act, but in the meantime the Spanish Government has not just passed such legislation, but got it up and running. We will be pressing our Government to show similar commitment to finding solutions.

In the meantime, even though revenues have continued to fall overall, there are some positive signs for the future. The UK digital market continues to grow strongly. 20% of the population downloaded music legally last year and retail spend total in this market since 2004 has now passed £1bn. Digital now accounts for over a third of industry income, with the 15 most-downloaded albums in 2011 all selling over 100,000 copies and revenue streams from areas such as subscription streaming services comprising a larger part of the mix. Of the new services on the horizon, Cloud-based storage services are the most-talked about, and major locker services from Google, Amazon and iTunes have the potential to add to industry revenues – but only if the Government does not destroy this new market before it has to chance to grow by enacting a private copying exception exempting many lockers from the need to get a licence. BPI has engaged very actively with Government over the last year to persuade it that the key to growth is providing the UK's creative industries with a strong copyright framework, not watering it down to benefit foreign tech companies.

Despite all the talk of digital, we must not forget that physical formats still account for the greatest share of our business. Although downloads constitute over 99% of sales in the singles market, over three quarters of albums bought in 2011 were CDs. Bricks and mortar retailers are hugely important, a fact underlined by the equity stake deal struck between HMV and some of its major suppliers at the beginning of this year. The loss of millions of pounds worth of stock at the Sony DADC distribution centre in the August riots also prompted a cross-industry response, with BPI establishing a fund to help affected labels experiencing financial difficulties. The CD is still the first-choice format for the majority of UK music buyers, and BPI is conducting research with the Entertainment Retailers Association to help labels in adding value into physical formats for the future.

The BPI's work spans many other issues. Throughout the year, work continued to make the Internet a safer place for young aspiring musicians and music fans to share and consume the music they enjoy. The Parental Advisory Scheme was updated to apply to digital services to ensure that music which might be inappropriate for young people is clearly labelled as Explicit or with the Parental Advisory logo. In the months ahead, we'll be aiming to add to the 20 services on board, generate additional material for our bespoke parental advisory website, and explore software products that would offer a comprehensive filtering solution to parents.

The BPI also accepted the Government's invitation to run a nationwide music competition for 11-19 year olds in 2011. From summer onwards, the competition – christened Next BRIT Thing – encouraged young people to write and record their own performances and upload them. With support from mainstream artists, Next BRIT Thing culminated in a series of regional auditions and a national final at the IndigO2 in March 2012, with judges McFly, Laura Wright and Noah Stewart. The competition was a great success in its first year and I was astonished at the quality and enthusiasm of the entrants. We are hoping to be able to run the competition again in future years.

With British performers accounting for the world's biggest selling artist album in four of the last five years, I am confident that the heart of our business – developing and nurturing talent – beats as strongly as ever. But the market for recorded music continues to evolve and develop at a breathtaking pace – both on the high street and online. It is more important than ever to keep abreast of the key statistics, trends and developments. BPI's Yearbook aims to be an invaluable tool for everyone involved in the business of creating and selling music and we hope you find this new edition to be as informative and useful as ever.

Geoff Taylor
Chief Executive, BPI

Industry Income

Digital now accounts for more than a third of industry income

BPI's survey of industry income was previously known as the trade deliveries survey. This has been expanded and now includes much more detail on downloads, mobile, subscription and ad-supported income. This provides a much better understanding of how record company income streams are diversifying in the digital age.

ANNUAL SUMMARY

Record industry revenue is diversifying. The market for digital music has been generating meaningful revenues now for eight years and as the graph to the right shows, more than a third of income now comes from digital sources.

This revenue goes beyond 'purchase to own' downloads and as the table on the facing page shows there are eight income streams within the digital sector covered by BPI's survey.

The growth in digital revenues accelerated in 2011 but a small decrease in total industry income was recorded for the year as a whole. Overall, trade revenues totalled £795.4m in 2011, a decrease of 3.4%.

Digital revenues grew by almost 25% in 2011, reaching £282m, which compares to a rise of just less than 20% in 2010. This is highly encouraging for the long term development of the digital music market in the UK, as a higher proportion of physical losses are now being offset by rising digital revenues. In 2011, two thirds of the decrease in physical format income was taken up by digital compared to only 26% in 2010.

Digital albums demonstrated the largest increase in monetary terms, generating £117.8m, £35.5m more than in 2010, an increase of 43.2%. In doing so, digital albums almost caught single track revenue which currently stands at £120.5m.

Losses in the **physical format** sector were £84m in absolute terms, down by 14.1% in 2011. Despite this CD albums are still the industry's largest format sector and accounted for more than 60% of total industry turnover in 2011.

Music video performed the best of all physical formats in 2011. Over the year, revenues from music video were down by only 3.3% compared to 14.4% for albums and 33.1% for physical format singles, which have now dwindled to only £3.3m.

Subscription is growing in importance. The success of Spotify and other services in migrating users from free tier services into paid subscribers is producing meaningful results. This channel generated more than £23m in 2011, 8.3% of digital income. There have been several media stories in the past 12 months about the non-availability of some high profile releases on such services (and on free ad-supported versions too), but clearly consumer demand is still strong as revenue grew by 43%.

Ad-supported, or free streaming, services' contribution to industry revenue was relatively flat last year, increasing slightly to £11.4m. This revenue includes income from free streaming services such as YouTube as well as from the free tiers of services such as Spotify and we7.

Sales of music video downloads, master ringtones and ringback tunes have failed to match the growth of other digital sectors in recent years. Their combined revenue was worth slightly more than £5m in 2011.

	2008	2009	2010	2011
Physical Formats	86.0%	79.7%	72.6%	64.6%
Online	12.0%	17.5%	23.5%	30.3%
Subscriptions	0.9%	1.3%	2.0%	2.9%
Ad-supported	0.3%	0.9%	1.3%	1.4%
Mobile	0.7%	0.4%	0.4%	0.3%
Other Digital	0.1%	0.2%	0.2%	0.4%
Total	100%	100%	100%	100%

Source: BPI Surveys

Digital's Share of Industry Revenues

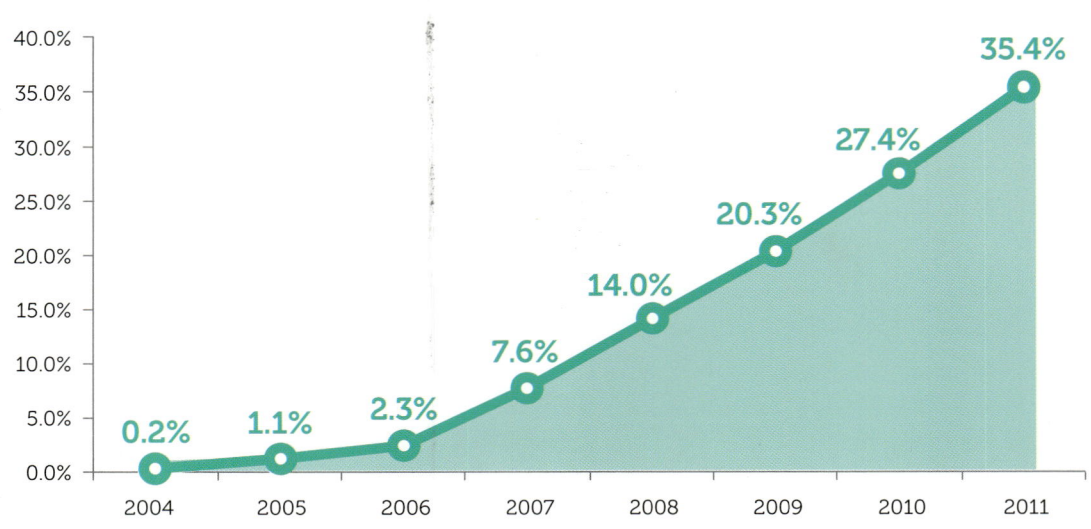

Year	Share
2004	0.2%
2005	1.1%
2006	2.3%
2007	7.6%
2008	14.0%
2009	20.3%
2010	27.4%
2011	35.4%

Source: BPI Surveys

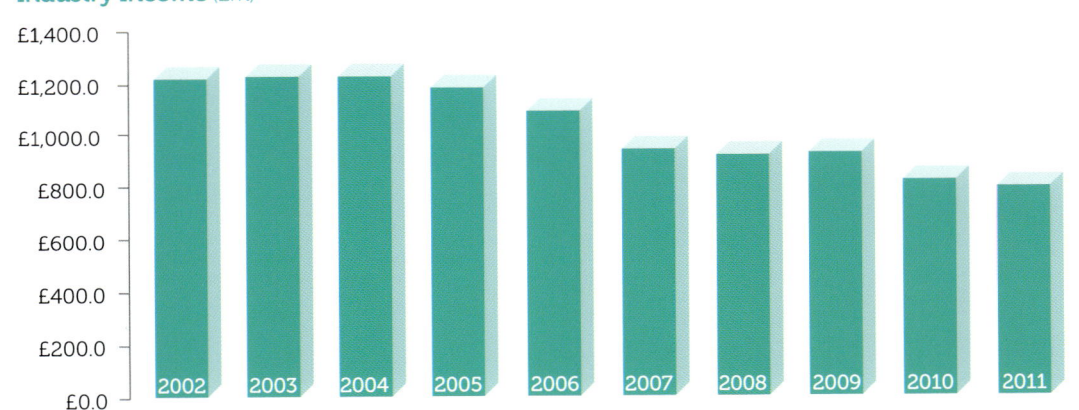

Industry Income (£m)

Source: BPI Surveys

£282m
DIGITAL REVENUES IN 2011

Industry Income (£m)

		2002	2003	2004	2005	2006	2007	2008	2009	2010	2011	% change
Physical Formats	Singles	£97.2	£64.5	£52.8	£43.1	£31.8	£19.0	£10.2	£7.6	£4.9	£3.3	-33.1%
	Albums	£1,089.0	£1,112.0	£1,102.2	£1,057.3	£982.9	£815.6	£749.1	£699.2	£566.4	£484.7	-14.4%
	Music Video	£23.5	£46.6	£62.7	£63.3	£49.1	£37.2	£28.5	£33.1	£26.7	£25.8	-3.3%
	Total	£1,209.7	£1,223.1	£1,217.7	£1,163.7	£1,063.8	£871.8	£787.8	£740.0	£598.0	£513.8	-14.1%
Online	Tracks	-	-	£2.7	£12.4	£25.2	£40.9	£62.5	£91.8	£108.3	£120.5	+11.3%
	Albums	-	-	-	-	-	£30.7	£43.7	£67.3	£82.2	£117.8	+43.2%
	Music video	-	-	-	-	-	-	£4.0	£3.4	£3.0	£2.8	-7.0%
	Total	-	-	£2.7	£12.4	£25.2	£71.6	£110.1	£162.6	£193.5	£241.1	+24.6%
Mobile	Master Ringtones	-	-	-	-	-	-	£5.3	£3.7	£3.3	£2.3	-32.0%
	Ringback Tunes	-	-	-	-	-	-	£0.8	£0.4	£0.3	£0.2	-14.4%
	Total	-	-	-	-	-	-	£6.0	£4.1	£3.6	£2.5	-30.6%
Subscriptions		-	-	-	-	-	-	£8.6	£11.8	£16.3	£23.3	+43.2%
Ad-supported		-	-	-	-	-	-	£2.4	£8.2	£10.8	£11.4	+5.1%
Other Digital Music Content		-	-	-	-	-	-	£0.8	£2.1	£1.6	£3.4	+105.8%
	Total	£1,209.7	£1,223.1	£1,220.4	£1,176.1	£1,089.0	£943.4	£915.6	£928.8	£823.8	£795.4	-3.4%

Source: BPI Surveys
Note: for the years 2004-2007 digital income was estimated on the basis of Official Charts Company retail volumes. Values are at wholesale, do not include VAT and are net of returns.

Retail Sales by Format – Albums

Digital sales grow by 27% in 2011

Sales of albums fell by 5.6% in 2011, dropping from just under 120m to 113.2m. The CD remains the favoured format for album buyers, accounting for 76.1% of total sales, but its continued decline was not offset by the growing appetite for downloads in the market. That said, digital is becoming an increasingly mainstream proposition – 15 albums sold over 100,000 digital copies in 2011 and sales in this sector grew by 26.6% to 26.6m, representing 23.5% of all albums bought. There was particularly strong demand at the close of the year, when over 1m digital albums were sold in one week for the first time. The biggest selling digital album of the year – by some distance – was **Adele**'s *21*, with almost 720,000 downloads.

The vinyl success story continued in 2011, with sales up to their highest level since 2005 and a fourth straight year of growth recorded. While still very much a minority format – its 0.3% market share equated to 337,000 sales – its devoted and broadening audience is making initiatives such as Record Store Day a great success.

The remaining minority formats (including cassette, DVD Audio, DVD Video, DMD and 7" vinyl box sets) together comprised 0.1% of sales.

15

NUMBER OF ALBUMS SELLING OVER 100,000 COPIES DIGITALLY IN 2011

Retail Sales by Format (units, thousands) – Albums

	2005	2006	2007	2008	2009	2010	2011	% change
CD	158,310	151,415	131,417	122,973	112,485	98,545	86,177	-12.6%
LP	351	251	205	209	219	234	337	+43.7%
Digital*	–	2,799	6,249	10,309	16,096	21,023	26,615	+26.6%
Other album formats**	328	278	194	153	147	104	57	-45.2%
Total	158,989	154,743	138,065	133,644	128,947	119,907	113,186	-5.6%

Format Split (units %)

	2005	2006	2007	2008	2009	2010	2011
CD	99.6	97.8	95.2	92.0	87.2	82.2	76.1
LP	0.2	0.2	0.1	0.2	0.2	0.2	0.3
Digital*	–	1.8	4.5	7.7	12.5	17.5	23.5
Other album formats**	0.2	0.2	0.1	0.1	0.1	0.1	0.1
Total	100	100	100	100	100	100	100

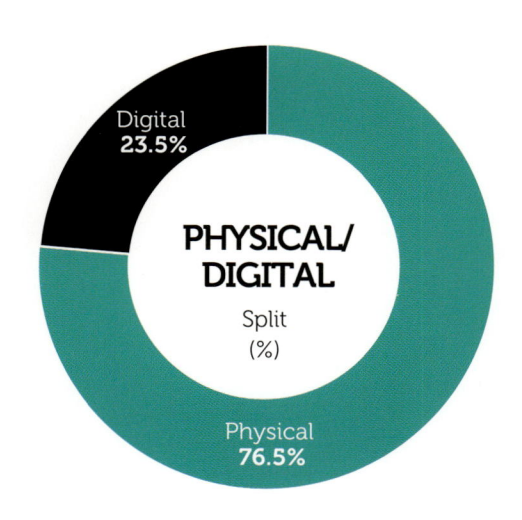

Source: Official Charts Company
*Digital represents nine months sales April-Dec 2006; full years from then on
**Other album formats include cassette, MiniDisc, DVD Audio, DVD Video, DMD and albums released as 7" single box sets

PHYSICAL/DIGITAL Split (%)
Digital 23.5%
Physical 76.5%

Retail Sales by Format – Singles

Sales record broken again

The singles market reached another annual sales peak in 2011, with the 177.9m sold a 10.0% improvement on 2010's record high. This was the eighth consecutive year of growth, with the 2011 sales tally almost six times that recorded in 2003 at the market's lowest point.

Digital – in the form of both single track downloads and bundles – continues to drive the market, with non-physical formats accounting for 99.3% of all sales, up from 98.7% the previous year. The entire year-end top 20 sold over half a million copies each in 2011, although the main format for one title – Military Wives & Gareth Malone's *Wherever You Are* – was CD, which accounted for almost 70% of its total. Despite this success, CD single sales dropped by over 40% to 1.1m, resulting in the format's share falling to below 1%.

In contrast to the albums market, vinyl's fortunes are declining – together, seven and twelve inch sales comprise only 0.1% of the market, slipping to below 200,000 across both. The diminishing role of physical formats in the singles sector meant that of the top 100 selling titles of the year, only four (by **Military Wives**, **Little Mix**, **One Direction** and **The Wanted**) had non-digital formats accounting for more than 5% of their sales.

10% GROWTH IN SINGLES SALES IN 2011

Retail Sales by Format (units, thousands) – Singles

	2005	2006	2007	2008	2009	2010	2011	% change
7"	1,073	1,046	1,040	486	222	152	123	-19.1%
12"	2,076	1,252	803	254	110	67	63	-5.6%
CD	17,523	11,312	6,633	4,075	2,470	1,857	1,106	-40.5%
Single Track Downloads	26,392	52,505	77,545	109,769	148,792	158,593	175,108	+10.4%
Digital Bundles	52	593	411	505	860	1,122	1,499	+33.6%
Other*	766	217	130	50	295	20	14	-28.7%
Total	47,882	66,925	86,562	115,139	152,749	161,811	177,914	+10.0%

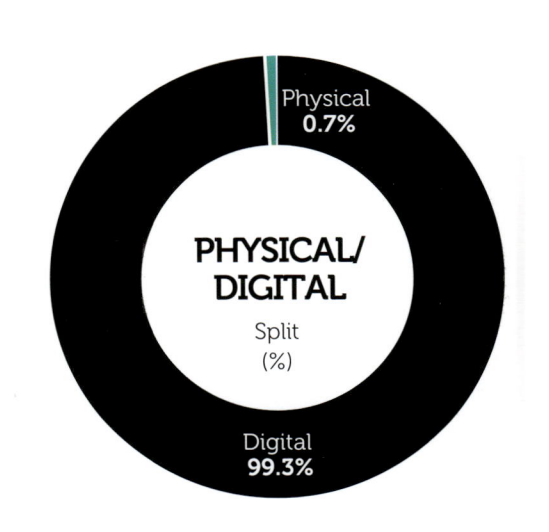

Format Split (units %)

	2005	2006	2007	2008	2009	2010	2011
7"	2.2	1.6	1.2	0.4	0.1	0.1	0.1
12"	4.3	1.9	0.9	0.2	0.1	-	-
CD	36.6	16.9	7.7	3.5	1.6	1.1	0.6
Single Track Downloads	55.1	78.5	89.6	95.3	97.4	98.0	98.4
Digital Bundles	0.1	0.9	0.5	0.4	0.6	0.7	0.8
Other*	1.6	0.3	0.2	-	0.2	-	-
Total	100	100	100	100	100	100	100

Source: Official Charts Company
*Other formats include DVD, DMD and cassette singles

PHYSICAL/DIGITAL Split (%)
Physical 0.7%
Digital 99.3%

Best Selling Albums

Record breaking year for Adele

To risk stating the obvious, 2011 was undoubtedly **Adele**'s year. By the end of it her **21** album had sold the largest amount ever in one calendar year – 3.8m – and shot straight to the top of the 21st century best sellers list ahead of **Amy Winehouse**'s **Back To Black**. After entering the chart at number one upon its release at the end of January it spent the next eleven weeks there and did not drop out of the top two until August. Her first album **19** also enjoyed a real revival, ending the year as the fourth biggest selling album and pushing her combined sales total up to 5m.

While the attention was undoubtedly focussed on these great achievements, a number of other artists connected with the public on a grand scale too. **Michael Bublé** followed up his great 2010 by releasing a new album – **Christmas** – that sold 1.3m copies in just 10 weeks, while **Bruno Mars** had the biggest debut of the year, his **Doo-Wops and Hooligans** clearing 1.2m and providing the American singer-songwriter with a run of hit singles.

As will be explored later in the book there was also a strong British presence in the top 20, with artists such as **Jessie J** and **Ed Sheeran** charting well with their debuts.

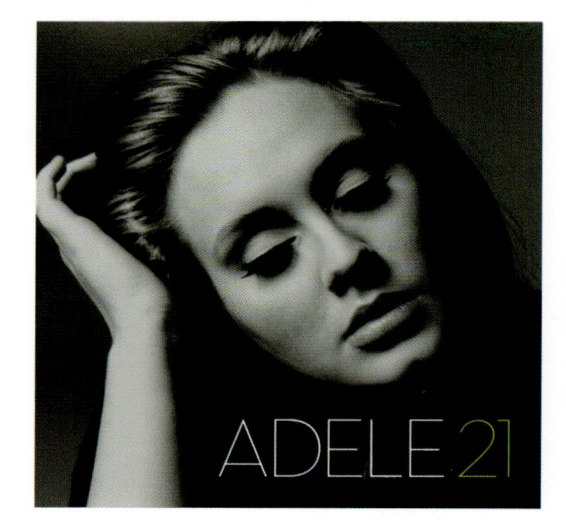

Top 20 Best Selling Albums 2011

1	Adele	21	XL Recordings
2	Michael Bublé	Christmas	Warner Bros
3	Bruno Mars	Doo-Wops & Hooligans	Atlantic Records UK
4	Adele	19	XL Recordings
5	Various Artists	Now That's What I Call Music 80	EMI TV/UMTV
6	Coldplay	Mylo Xyloto	Parlophone
7	Rihanna	Loud	Mercury
8	Various Artists	Now That's What I Call Music 79	EMI TV/UMTV
9	Lady Gaga	Born This Way	Polydor
10	Jessie J	Who You Are	Universal Island
11	Ed Sheeran	+	Atlantic Records UK
12	Various Artists	Now That's What I Call Music 78	EMI TV/UMTV
13	Rihanna	Talk That Talk	Mercury
14	Amy Winehouse	Lioness – Hidden Treasures	Universal Island
15	Olly Murs	In Case You Didn't Know	Epic Label Group
16	Cee Lo Green	The Lady Killer	Warner Bros
17	Noel Gallagher's High Flying Birds	Noel Gallagher's High Flying Birds	Sour Mash
18	Take That	Progress	Polydor
19	One Direction	Up All Night	RCA Label Group
20	Chase & Status	No More Idols	Mercury

Source: Official Charts Company

Best Selling Singles

Adele and Maroon 5 tracks top 1m sales

Whereas no singles reached the one million sales marker in 2010, two did so in 2011. **Adele**'s *Someone Like You* raced to the top of the singles chart after an astonishing performance at the BRIT Awards in February and stayed there for the next three weeks, selling a remarkable 1.2m copies by the end of the year. Released in August, **Maroon 5**'s *Moves Like Jagger* never made it to number one but spent a total of 12 weeks in the top five and crossed the 1m sales line in the last week of 2011. **LMFAO**'s *Party Rock Anthem* only just missed out on passing the million sales mark, reaching the total in the first week of the new year.

There were several parallels with the best selling albums list. Two titles by **Adele** featured in the top 10, with **Jessie J** and **Ed Sheeran** both featuring for the first time. **Bruno Mars** and **Rihanna** also featured in both top 10s, the former's *Grenade* topping the chart in January, while *We Found Love* gave **Rihanna** a number one single in October.

Among those featuring for the first time in the year-end top 20 were the American singer-songwriter **Christina Perri** (with *Jar Of Hearts*) and **Aloe Blacc**, whose *I Need A Dollar* peaked at number two in May.

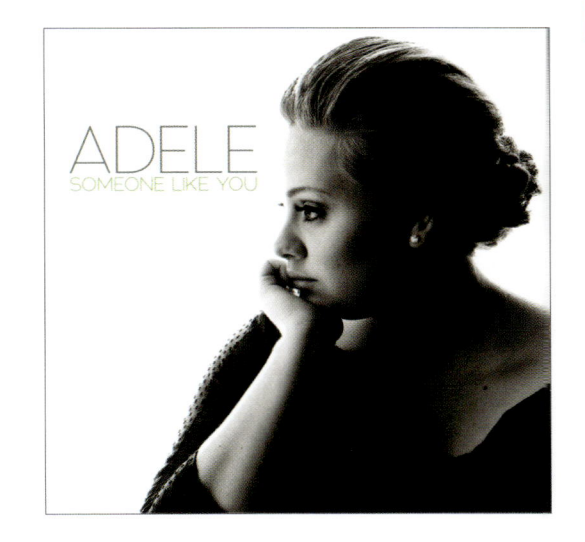

Top 20 Best Selling Singles 2011

1	Adele	Someone Like You	XL Recordings
2	Maroon 5 ft Christina Aguilera	Moves Like Jagger	Polydor
3	LMFAO/Lauren Bennett/Goonrock	Party Rock Anthem	Polydor
4	Jessie J ft Bob	Price Tag	Universal Island
5	Rihanna ft Calvin Harris	We Found Love	Mercury
6	Pitbull/Ne-Yo/Afrojack/Nayer	Give Me Everything	RCA Label Group
7	Bruno Mars	Grenade	Atlantic Records UK
8	Ed Sheeran	The A Team	Atlantic Records UK
9	Adele	Rolling In The Deep	XL Recordings
10	Jennifer Lopez ft Pitbull	On The Floor	Mercury
11	Christina Perri	Jar Of Hearts	Atlantic Records UK
12	Rihanna	S&M	Mercury
13	Military Wives/Gareth Malone	Wherever You Are	Decca
14	Lady Gaga	Born This Way	Polydor
15	Bruno Mars	The Lazy Song	Atlantic Records UK
16	Chris Brown ft Benny Benassi	Beautiful People	RCA Label Group
17	Example	Changed The Way You Kiss Me	Ministry Of Sound
18	Aloe Blacc	I Need A Dollar	Epic Label Group
19	Snoop Dogg	Sweat	Parlophone
20	One Direction	What Makes You Beautiful	RCA Label Group

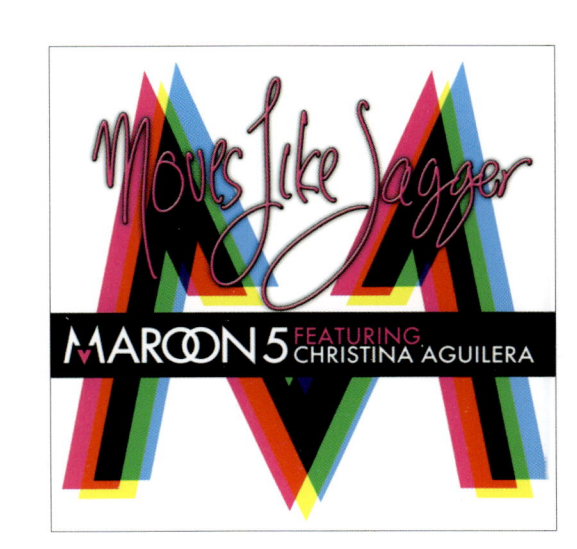

Source: Official Charts Company

Sales by Artist Nationality – Albums

UK takes biggest share this century

Propelled by the success of **Adele**, along with big selling albums by artists such as **Coldplay**, **Jessie J**, **Ed Sheeran** and **Olly Murs**, British artists were responsible for 52.7% of album sales in 2011.

This was the UK's biggest share of the domestic market since 1997. In that year British acts notched up a 58.3% share and took the top five places in the annual chart, **Oasis** scoring the top seller with **Be Here Now**. While 2011's achievement was not quite on that scale – five of the top 10 artist albums were by British acts – it does signify something of a revival, with UK share below 50% for the previous three years.

Over half (56) of the top 100 albums were by UK artists, ranging from those on their debuts (**The Vaccines**, **Katy B**, **Rizzle Kicks**) to new albums from more established acts (**Will Young**, **PJ Harvey**, **Kasabian**).

The US took a slightly smaller share in 2011, with its biggest sellers coming from **Bruno Mars**, **Lady Gaga** and **Cee Lo Green**. Canada again took a strong 4.5% share, contributed to by successes from **Michael Bublé**, **Drake** and **Justin Bieber**, while **Rihanna** was the sole contributor to Barbados's 2.3%, who overtook Ireland to move into fourth place in the share table.

France's best share this century was largely attributable to **David Guetta**, who had two titles feature in the artist albums top 100, while strong sales from **Andrea Bocelli** helped Italy claim an improved 0.4%.

52.7%
SHARE OF ALBUM SALES TAKEN BY UK ARTISTS IN 2011

UK Album Sales by Country of Artist's Origin (% units)

	2007	2008	2009	2010	2011
UK	51.9	49.1	48.8	48.9	52.7
USA	34.4	35.3	37.5	35.8	32.7
Canada	3.8	3.5	3.3	4.5	4.5
Barbados	0.7	1.0	0.5	1.6	2.3
Ireland	2.5	2.6	3.1	2.6	2.2
Netherlands	0.1	0.1	0.1	1.2	1.1
France	0.4	0.5	0.5	0.6	0.9
Australia	1.1	1.6	1.7	1.9	0.7
Sweden	0.6	1.5	0.9	0.5	0.5
Italy	0.9	0.6	0.5	0.2	0.4
Germany	0.9	0.9	0.6	0.5	0.3
Jamaica	0.5	0.5	0.3	0.2	0.3
Spain	0.4	0.7	0.3	0.2	0.2
New Zealand	0.2	0.2	0.3	0.1	0.2
Denmark	0.1	0.4	0.2	0.1	0.1
Iceland	0.2	0.3	0.1	0.1	0.1
Switzerland	-	0.1	-	-	0.1
Finland	0.1	0.1	0.1	0.1	0.1
Norway	0.1	-	0.1	0.1	0.1
Mexico	0.1	-	-	0.1	0.1
Other	1.0	1.0	1.1	0.7	0.4
Total	100	100	100	100	100

Source: BPI analysis based on Official Charts Company sales data

Coldplay

Sales by Artist Nationality – Singles

US artists top the table again in 2011

Sales of singles by American artists comprised the greatest share in the market for a third year running in 2011, rising to 43.8% from 43.0% in 2010. Five of the top 10 sellers were by US acts, with **Maroon 5**'s ***Moves Like Jagger*** the top American seller, although the presence of four **Bruno Mars** tracks in the year-end top 75 was another major contributing factor to the US's success.

The UK's share increased to its highest level in three years, helped by **Adele** (who had two tracks in the Top 10) as well as artists such as **One Direction**, **Jessie J** and **Ed Sheeran**, who all released singles that sold over half a million copies. Further UK successes came from **Military Wives** and **Example**, who both had singles feature in the 2011 top 20.

Barbados climbed one place in the rankings to third, taking a 3.8% share thanks not only to **Rihanna** but **Cover Drive**, whose ***Lick Ya Down*** was a top 10 hit in August. France took fourth place, with **David Guetta**'s multiple hits (four tracks in the Top 100) helping more than double their share to 2.4%. Romania also built on their 2010 share with **Alexandra Stan**'s ***Mr Saxobeat*** selling over half a million copies across the year, while Spain's best result since 2007 was aided by **Sak Noel**, whose ***Loca People*** was a number one in September and sold over a quarter of a million.

43.8%
SHARE OF SINGLES MARKET CLAIMED BY US ACTS IN 2011

UK Singles Sales by Country of Artist's Origin (% units)

	2007	2008	2009	2010	2011
USA	36.9	38.7	44.1	43.0	43.8
UK	47.3	43.7	42.3	40.7	42.6
Barbados	2.1	2.5	0.8	2.5	3.8
France	0.9	0.2	1.5	1.1	2.4
Canada	3.7	2.7	1.5	2.4	1.5
Sweden	1.6	3.3	1.5	1.2	1.0
Romania	-	-	-	0.8	0.9
Spain	0.9	0.3	0.4	0.6	0.8
Ireland	1.1	1.8	1.2	1.3	0.7
Netherlands	1.2	0.2	0.4	0.7	0.6
Australia	1.0	2.9	2.4	2.5	0.5
Jamaica	0.1	0.2	0.1	0.3	0.4
Italy	0.3	0.2	0.1	0.2	0.4
Colombia	0.2	0.1	0.5	0.4	0.2
Denmark	0.4	0.8	0.2	0.1	0.1
Norway	-	0.4	0.3	0.1	0.1
New Zealand	-	-	-	-	0.1
Other	2.3	2.0	2.7	2.1	0.1
Total	100	100	100	100	100

Source: BPI analysis based on Official Charts Company sales data

Bruno Mars

Sales by Type of Music – Albums

Pop replaces Rock as most popular genre

Pop artists dominated the upper reaches of the chart with seven of the top 10 best sellers of the year classified as such, including titles by **Bruno Mars**, **Lady Gaga** and **Jessie J**. As a result, Pop's share increased from 30.9% to over a third of the market (33.6%), its highest since 1999, and overtook Rock in the process.

Rock's share of sales fell to its lowest in eight years, dipping below 30% for the first time since 2003. There was a distinct lack of big sellers in 2011, with **Coldplay** and **Noel Gallagher's High Flying Birds** the only artists from the genre to have titles placed in the combined top 20.

The huge success of **Michael Buble's** *Christmas* album (the second biggest seller of the year) gave the MOR genre a boost in 2011, its share rising from 7.5% to 7.9%. There were also solid sales from artists such as **Susan Boyle**, **Rumer** and **Alfie Boe**.

Dance, Hip Hop and Classical all saw their share of sales fall, although Folk's rose to its highest of the century, with popular titles from artists such as **Laura Marling** and **Bellowhead** helping it up to 1.6%. Blues also had something of a banner year thanks to new albums from **Hugh Laurie** and **Seasick Steve**.

Album Sales by Genre (% units)

	2002	2003	2004	2005	2006	2007	2008	2009	2010	2011
Pop	30.3	31.2	27.9	19.8	20.8	22.3	25.3	29.0	30.9	33.6
Rock	31.0	29.2	30.8	40.0	41.5	37.2	35.7	31.0	31.2	29.4
R&B	7.4	8.4	8.8	7.6	8.7	10.3	10.5	9.6	10.4	10.1
MOR/Easy Listening	6.1	6.4	7.1	8.1	6.9	7.0	7.2	8.2	7.5	7.9
Dance	9.5	7.2	7.0	8.3	7.7	8.1	7.9	7.3	5.8	4.9
Hip Hop	5.1	5.5	6.4	5.6	3.2	2.7	2.2	4.3	4.2	3.4
Classical	3.5	3.8	3.4	3.3	3.4	3.6	3.7	3.2	3.5	3.3
Country	1.5	1.8	2.0	1.3	2.2	2.4	1.8	1.6	1.4	1.6
Folk	1.4	1.2	1.2	1.2	1.2	1.2	1.2	1.4	1.3	1.6
Jazz	2.0	2.6	3.2	2.1	1.9	2.4	1.7	1.5	1.6	1.5
Blues	0.3	0.3	0.4	0.3	0.3	0.4	0.5	0.7	0.6	0.9
Reggae	0.7	1.5	0.9	1.0	0.7	0.8	0.8	0.9	0.6	0.7
Childrens	0.3	0.2	0.2	0.5	0.5	0.8	0.5	0.4	0.4	0.4
World	0.4	0.5	0.5	0.5	0.6	0.6	0.5	0.4	0.4	0.3
Spoken Word	0.1	0.1	0.2	0.2	0.1	0.2	0.2	0.3	0.1	0.1
New Age	0.1	0.2	0.1	0.3	0.2	0.1	0.3	0.2	0.1	0.1
Total	100	100	100	100	100	100	100	100	100	100

Source: BPI based on Official Charts Company data

Sales by Type of Music – Singles

Rock's share improves but Pop remains top

Pop's share of singles sales decreased slightly in 2011, but was still twice as large as that of Rock. The two biggest sellers of the year (by **Adele** and **Maroon 5**) were both Pop tracks as were 37 of the top 100. Only six of the top 100 tracks were classed as Rock (the biggest selling was **Coldplay**'s *Paradise* at number 21) but the sheer weight of the genre's back catalogue ensured that its share did not fade – in fact it increased slightly, resulting in it leapfrogging R&B for the second spot.

Dance polled its best share in five years in 2011, claiming 13.8% of sales. One factor contributing to this rise (and the attendant decrease in R&B) was the growing number of tracks allocated to this genre by Urban artists.

The cross-pollination of the two genres has been one of the big trends in the past year, and among Dance's biggest sellers were tracks by **Rihanna**, **Chris Brown** and **Snoop Dogg**.

Classical's share rose very sharply, with much of the increase attributable to the success of the single by **Military Wives & Gareth Malone**, which was not only the Christmas number one but the fastest seller of the year.

MOR/Easy also recorded sizeable share growth, taking over 1% of sales for the first time since 2001. Tracks by **Michael Bublé**, **Rumer** and **Eva Cassidy** were among the best sellers.

Singles Sales by Genre (% units)

	2002	2003	2004	2005	2006	2007	2008	2009	2010	2011
Pop	51.8	38.3	35.0	28.0	19.4	19.6	28.1	33.5	38.3	36.0
Rock	13.4	17.1	17.2	29.7	35.3	37.0	31.2	24.5	17.2	18.0
R&B	7.6	15.9	14.9	13.5	17.7	17.8	18.3	18.9	18.0	17.2
Dance	15.4	15.3	17.8	15.4	18.2	15.5	13.2	12.7	12.6	13.8
Hip Hop	10.0	11.1	13.7	11.8	8.3	8.1	7.7	8.8	12.2	10.2
MOR/Easy	0.9	0.4	-	0.3	0.2	0.9	0.5	0.7	0.8	1.4
Classical	-	-	-	-	-	0.1	-	0.1	0.1	1.2
Reggae	0.2	1.2	0.6	1.0	0.6	0.2	0.2	0.2	0.3	0.6
Folk	-	-	-	-	-	0.1	0.2	0.1	0.1	0.6
Country	0.5	0.7	0.1	0.1	0.1	0.3	0.3	0.3	0.2	0.5
Jazz	-	-	0.6	0.2	0.1	0.4	0.3	0.3	0.2	0.3
Other	0.2	-	0.1	-	0.1	-	-	-	-	0.3
Total	100	100	100	100	100	100	100	100	100	100

Source: BPI based on Official Charts Company data

Genre Focus – Pop

Album sales share: 33.6% (1st)
Singles sales share: 36.0% (1st)

Although **Adele**'s huge success was undoubtedly a key contributing factor to Pop's success in 2011, it shouldn't be overlooked that – aside from **Adele**'s two albums – there were another five Pop titles in the combined albums top 10 for the year. The 2011-released albums by **Ed Sheeran**, **Amy Winehouse** and **Olly Murs** all sold over half a million copies, with new titles by **One Direction**, **Rebecca Ferguson** and **The Wanted** also selling strongly. In total, 45 of the top 100 albums of the year were classified as Pop, up from 43 in 2010.

Pop's share can be split into three constituent parts. The main Pop sub-genre always makes up the biggest, representing 31.6% of the entire albums market in 2011, while Karaoke claims the smallest share (0.1% for the past five years). Rock & Roll is responsible for the remainder of the sales attributed to Pop, accumulating an improved 1.9% of total album sales in 2011 thanks to big sellers from **The Overtones** and **Imelda May**.

Pop Album Sales by Sub-Genre (% units, down)

	2009	2010	2011
Pop	27.7	29.1	31.6
Rock & Roll	1.2	1.7	1.9
Karaoke	0.1	0.1	0.1
Total	29.0	30.9	33.6

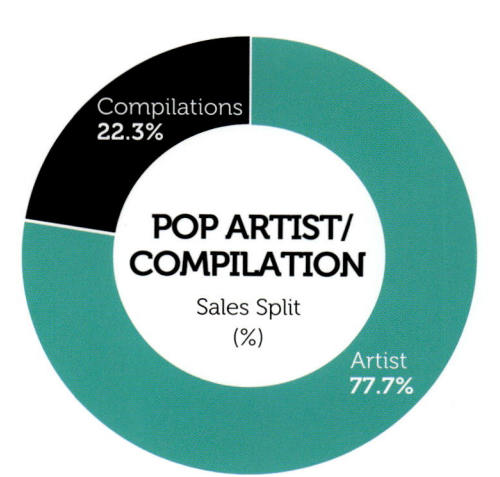

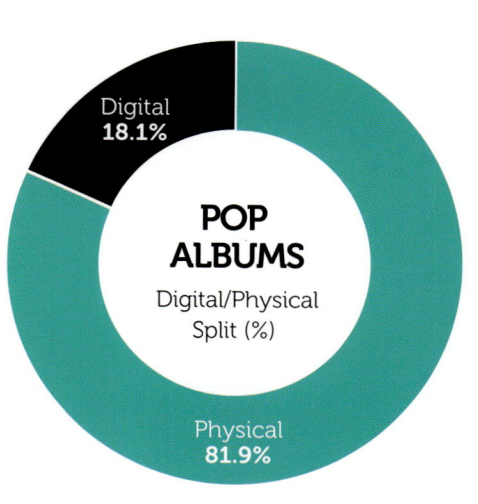

Source: BPI based on Official Charts Company data

POP ARTIST/COMPILATION Sales Split (%)
- Compilations 22.3%
- Artist 77.7%

POP ALBUMS Digital/Physical Split (%)
- Digital 18.1%
- Physical 81.9%

One Direction

Imelda May

TOP 10 BEST SELLERS

1	**ADELE** *21* XL Recordings	
2	**BRUNO MARS** *Doo-Wops & Hooligans* Atlantic Records UK	
3	**ADELE** *19* XL Recordings	
4	**VARIOUS ARTISTS** *Now That's What I Call Music 80* EMI TV/UMTV	
5	**VARIOUS ARTISTS** *Now That's What I Call Music 79* EMI TV/UMTV	
6	**LADY GAGA** *Born This Way* Polydor	
7	**JESSIE J** *Who You Are* Universal Island	
8	**ED SHEERAN** *+* Atlantic Records UK	
9	**VARIOUS ARTISTS** *Now That's What I Call Music 78* EMI TV/UMTV	
10	**AMY WINEHOUSE** *Lioness – Hidden Treasures* Universal Island	

Source: Official Charts Company

PROFILE:
Ed Sheeran's +

One of the biggest breakthrough artists of 2011 was **Ed Sheeran**, whose album + made the year-end top 10 best sellers list and, by March 2012, had sold over 1m copies.

"There are two key elements running through our campaign:" says **Managing Director of Asylum Records, Ben Cook**, "letting Ed's extraordinary talent speak for itself and expanding on his very genuine relationships with his fans.

Before he signed with us in January 2011, he'd self-released four EPs and built up a visceral core of fans, mainly 17 and 18 year olds. Outside of that core, there was awareness among his peer artists and generation but he wasn't yet well known. We were immediately struck by the strength of his songs and performances, both live and on places like SB:TV. There was a powerful sense of 'latency' in his generation: here is an artist who will break quickly, and he's going to be massive. Ed signed with us because he felt at home with some of the other artists we'd worked with and our 'culture' as a label, but above all he knew we respected his vision, and we had the same ambitions as he did for his future.

An early pivotal movement was the video we released of his remarkable live–looped acapella version of *Wayfaring Stranger*. After that, even before the first single, he was booked on Jools Holland and had incredibly influential support from Zane Lowe. When we arranged for Ed to play a free show at the Barfly in Camden, as a thank you to the fans, over 1,000 people turned up – he did three sets inside and one outside to make sure everyone who'd queued for hours had seen him.

It's that care, attention and generosity that is central to Ed's relationship with his fans. When we agreed that *The A Team* was going to be the lead single he tweeted to fans about the decision saying it would be deleted from a previous EP and he hoped everyone could support that decision. The reaction was great and the single went on to debut at number 3 and apparently was the longest serving track in the top 20 since *Love Is All Around* 20 years ago. *The A Team* really is a magical song. We followed up with *You Need Me...* and then *Lego House* and *Drunk*. Video is a crucial part of an artist's identity, and Ed was very involved in those promos, we've backed him creatively there too.

+ broke the record for first week digital album sales, which really said something about the fervent core audience who were buying it. Now in 12 months he's had four top 10 hits, and won two BRITs, and with one million album sales he's also striking a chord with people who maybe only buy two or three albums a year. The campaign has excited his original fans while taking his music to a massive mainstream audience. I feel that's because we've stayed true to who Ed is."

* THERE ARE TWO KEY ELEMENTS RUNNING THROUGH OUR CAMPAIGN: LETTING ED'S EXTRAORDINARY TALENT SPEAK FOR ITSELF AND EXPANDING ON HIS VERY GENUINE RELATIONSHIPS WITH HIS FANS. *

Genre Focus – Rock

Album sales share: 29.4% (2nd)
Singles sales share: 18.0% (2nd)

Rock's share of album sales rallied slightly in 2010 but the fall back to 29.4% in 2011 – aside from the obvious 'Adele effect' – can largely be attributed to a low number of new artists breaking through in the genre. Whereas Pop acts such as **Jessie J**, **Ed Sheeran** and **Bruno Mars** all made the year-end artist albums top 10 with their debuts, only three 2011-released Rock debuts (by **Noel Gallagher's High Flying Birds**, **The Vaccines** and **Beady Eye**) made the artist top 100.

Coldplay's *Mylo Xyloto* was the only Rock album to make the 2011 top 10, although new albums by **Florence & The Machine**, **Foo Fighters**, **Elbow** and **Kasabian** all sold more than a quarter of a million copies. In total, 18 Rock titles made the year-end top 100, compared with 26 a year earlier.

Rock's share of sales can be divided among four sub-genres – Contemporary, AOR, Metal/Punk and Progressive. Contemporary traditionally takes the largest, and did so again in 2011 (16.7% of all albums sold), while AOR's share dropped slightly, the biggest seller being **Bon Jovi**'s 2010-released *Greatest Hits*. Metal/Punk remained steady on 6.8% (**Foo Fighters** again the biggest selling act), with Progressive seeing a slight upturn thanks to the success of the **Pink Floyd** reissues.

Rock Album Sales by Sub-Genre
(% units, down)

	2009	2010	2011
Contemporary	18.5	16.5	16.7
AOR	5.3	7.2	5.0
Metal/Punk	6.6	6.8	6.8
Progressive	0.7	0.7	0.9
Total	31.0	31.2	29.4

Source: BPI based on Official Charts Company data

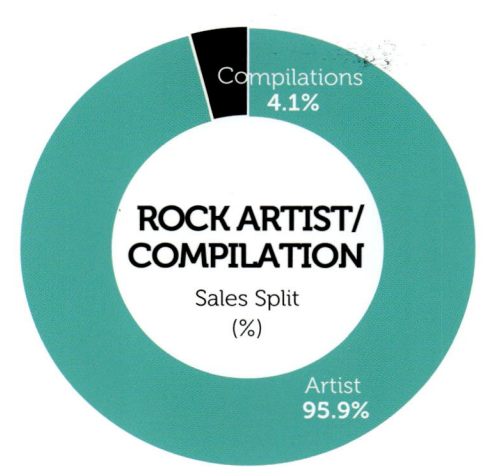

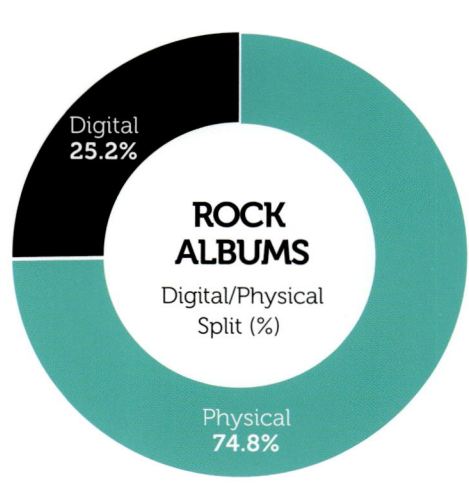

ROCK ARTIST/COMPILATION Sales Split (%)
- Compilations 4.1%
- Artist 95.9%

ROCK ALBUMS Digital/Physical Split (%)
- Digital 25.2%
- Physical 74.8%

TOP 10 BEST SELLERS

1 COLDPLAY
Mylo Xyloto
Parlophone

2 NOEL GALLAGHER'S HIGH FLYING BIRDS
Noel Gallagher's High Flying Birds
Sour Mash

3 FLORENCE & THE MACHINE
Ceremonials
Universal Island

4 FOO FIGHTERS
Wasting Light
Columbia Label Group

5 MUMFORD & SONS
Sigh No More
Universal Island

6 ELBOW
Build A Rocket Boys
Polydor

7 KASABIAN
Velociraptor
Columbia Label Group

8 SNOW PATROL
Fallen Empires
Polydor

9 NOAH & THE WHALE
Last Night On Earth
Mercury

10 ARCTIC MONKEYS
Suck It And See
Domino Recordings

Source: Official Charts Company

Rock Vinyl

TOP 10 ROCK BEST SELLERS – VINYL

1 RADIOHEAD
The King Of Limbs
XL Recordings

2 NOEL GALLAGHER'S HIGH FLYING BIRDS
Noel Gallagher's High Flying Birds
Sour Mash

3 PJ HARVEY
Let England Shake
Universal Island

4 ARCTIC MONKEYS
Suck It And See
Domino Recordings

5 BON IVER
Bon Iver
4AD

6 BEADY EYE
Different Gear Still Speeding
Beady Eye

7 ALEX TURNER
Submarine – OST
Domino Recordings

8 PINK FLOYD
Dark Side Of The Moon
Parlophone/Virgin

9 NIRVANA
Nevermind
Polydor

10 GORILLAZ
The Singles Collection 2001-2011
Parlophone

Source: Official Charts Company

There was again much interest in 2011 surrounding the continued growth of vinyl sales. After reaching a low of 205,000 in 2007 the annual total has risen every year since, with the 2011 figure of 337,000 meaning that not only are sales now at their highest since 2005 but that the market has increased in size by almost two thirds in just four years.

While in the context of recorded music sales as a whole these are relatively small numbers – vinyl only represents 0.3% of all albums sold – this market serves a passionate customer base that appears to be broadening with every year.

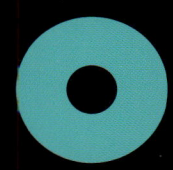

* ROCK IS THE DRIVING FORCE BEHIND THE VINYL REVIVAL AND SALES ARE AT THEIR HIGHEST LEVEL SINCE 2005. *

Although an increasing number of Pop titles are now being pressed on the format, Rock is very much the force behind its recent success. Of the 10 best selling vinyl titles in 2011, eight were classified as Rock, including the runaway best seller, **Radiohead**'s *The King Of Limbs*. With over 20,000 copies sold according to Official Charts Company data, it became the most popular vinyl title since **Travis**'s *The Invisible Band* and sold five times more than the second-placed title in the 2011 LP chart.

The very biggest sellers of the year were new releases but there is also a significant market for older titles. **Pink Floyd**'s classic *Dark Side Of The Moon* and **Nirvana**'s *Nevermind* were both issued on vinyl as part of deluxe reissue campaigns in 2011 and one of the biggest sellers on April's Record Store Day was the vinyl release of **The Smiths'** *The Queen Is Dead*.

Genre Focus – Urban

R&B:
Album sales share: 10.1% (3rd)
Singles sales share: 17.2% (3rd)

Hip Hop:
Album sales share: 3.4% (6th)
Singles sales share: 10.2% (5th)

Rihanna ruled the Urban market in 2011, her **Loud** album being the biggest seller in the genre for a second year running. She also claimed second place in the chart with her newer **Talk That Talk** set, released towards the end of November 2011 and by the end of the year she had sold more than 1.8m albums across her catalogue. Her success helped R&B's share of total album sales remain above 10% for a second year running, with albums such as **Cee Lo Green**'s **The Lady Killer** and **Plan B**'s **The Defamation Of Strickland Banks** among the titles to enjoy another year of solid sales.

Although the Urban chart was peppered with titles released before 2011, both **Chase and Status**'s **No More Idols** and **Beyonce**'s **4** proved that there would be big new releases to remember the year by. The London duo's second album gave them four hit singles and sold almost half a million copies in 2011, with some innovative marketing ensuring it remained in and around the top 20 for most of the year (see facing page). **Beyonce**'s album quickly followed her much talked-about debut Glastonbury performance and entered the charts at number one on its week of release in June.

The current structure of genre definition means that Contemporary Urban is divisible into four sub-genres: R&B, Hip Hop, Drum & Bass and UK Garage. In addition, Heritage Urban – otherwise known as Soul – is listed out as a separate genre. For the sake of simplicity in this analysis, Hip Hop has been listed on its own with everything else coming under the umbrella of R&B. Heritage Urban typically claims a share of around 1.5% of all album sales, driven chiefly by compilations and titles by artists such as **Stevie Wonder** and **Marvin Gaye**, while Drum & Bass and UK Garage's share can fluctuate to a great degree depending on whether a crossover album has been classified within either. In 2011 **No More Idols** was classed as Drum & Bass, while **Katy B**'s debut **On A Mission** was UK Garage, helping those sub-genres up to relatively high respective shares of 0.9% and 0.4%.

After two relatively solid years, Hip Hop's share of album sales fell back below 4% again in 2011. It still claimed above 10% in the singles market thanks to hits from artists such as **Professor Green**, **Labrinth** and **Flo Rida**, but a relative paucity of new releases meant that only two titles from the genre featured in the overall top 100 albums chart – in 2010 three titles charted in the top 40.

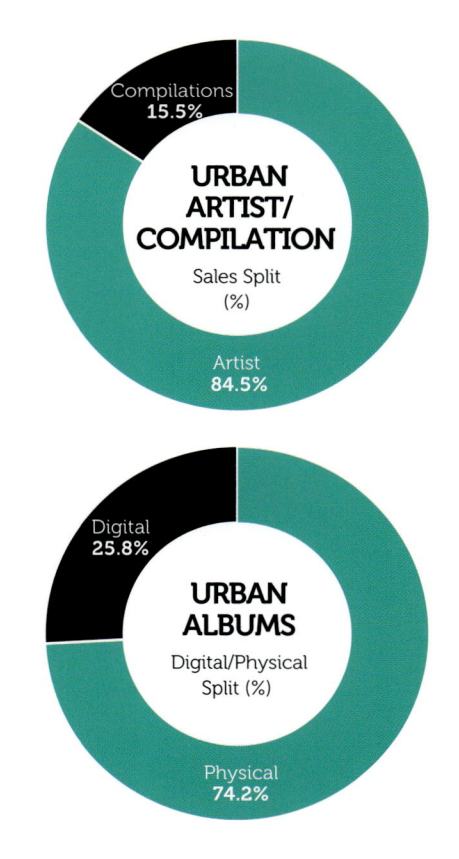

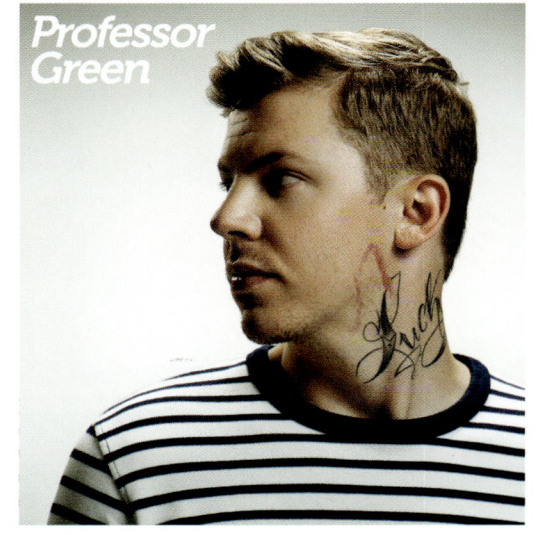

URBAN ARTIST/COMPILATION Sales Split (%)
Compilations 15.5%
Artist 84.5%

URBAN ALBUMS Digital/Physical Split (%)
Digital 25.8%
Physical 74.2%

TOP 10 BEST SELLERS

1. **RIHANNA**
   Loud
   Mercury

2. **RIHANNA**
   Talk That Talk
   Mercury

3. **CEE LO GREEN**
   The Lady Killer
   Warner Bros

4. **CHASE & STATUS**
   No More Idols
   Mercury

5. **BEYONCE**
   4
   RCA Label Group

6. **PLAN B**
   The Defamation Of Strickland Banks
   Atlantic Records UK

7. **TINIE TEMPAH**
   Disc-Overy
   Parlophone

8. **JLS**
   Jukebox
   Epic Label Group

9. **AMY WINEHOUSE**
   Back To Black
   Universal Island

10. **CHRIS BROWN**
    F.A.M.E.
    RCA Label Group

Source: Official Charts Company

PROFILE:

Chase and Status's *No More Idols*

The London-based production duo of Chase & Status scored a number two album in January 2011 with their second album *No More Idols*, which went on to become one of the 20 best sellers of the year.

"We already knew pretty much who their audience were – aged 16 to 24, with a slight male bias – from their gigs, Facebook and our own databases" says Mercury Records' **Michael Rivalland**. "It was evident to us it was a strong album with plenty of singles, so it was really about being innovative and thorough in reaching out to people throughout the campaign. We took out lots of digital ads, including things like expandable banner ads where you could mix album tracks and interact with the music. There were also some virals we broke some new ground with, such as a music video for *Let You Go* that users of Facebook could feature in. We also worked with iTunes on a '360' campaign – essentially a co-operative marketing partnership around the album, with ads placed on sites such as Facebook – which helped deliver a really strong digital share of almost 50% in its first week.

We made sure we covered the traditional bases with the marketing too. There was a comprehensive poster campaign, radio ads on Kiss, Capital and XFM and some TV spots as well, which got broader as the campaign progressed. We made two TV ads in the end – a more specialist one for launch and a broader, more aspirational one after the album went Platinum. Lots of emphasis was put on them as a live act, with footage from the various tours mixed in with the official videos."

* **IT WAS EVIDENT TO US IT WAS A STRONG ALBUM WITH PLENTY OF SINGLES, SO IT WAS REALLY ABOUT BEING INNOVATIVE AND THOROUGH IN REACHING OUT TO PEOPLE THROUGHOUT THE CAMPAIGN.** *

PROFILE: David Guetta's *Nothing But The Beat*

Over the past two years David Guetta has made the transition from one of the most popular and respected DJ/producers in Dance to arguably its biggest star outright. His *Nothing But The Beat* album sold well over a quarter of a million copies in 2011 and has now produced six top 10 hits, including the number one *Titanium*.

While Dance artists (and their audience) are often viewed as singles-centric, Guetta has now released two Platinum-selling albums in a row. He has also challenged the perception of Dance music producers as somewhat anonymous – Guetta is media-friendly and visibly engaged with his fans, with over 31m likes on his official Facebook page, more than 4m Twitter followers and in excess of a billion views of his videos across platforms such as YouTube and Vevo.

VIRGIN'S PLAN FOR NOTHING BUT THE BEAT WAS TO REINTRODUCE DAVID TO THE UK MEDIA AND MAINSTREAM AUDIENCE AS A POP MUSIC PERSONALITY AS WELL AS SERVE HIS CORE FOLLOWING OF DANCE FANS.

Tracks created with up and coming producers such as Afrojack and Avicii helped demonstrate he hadn't lost touch with the latter, while his collaborations with major league Urban and Pop artists (all with engaging, imaginative accompanying videos) helped position him with the more casual music fan. This duality was mirrored in the construction of the release itself – one disc contained only vocal collaborations, with instrumental material on the second.

Virgin's sales and marketing campaign has continued into 2012 and in March *Nothing But The Beat* climbed to number two, equalling its week of release chart peak, passing the 400,000 sales mark in the UK out of a global total of over 2.4m albums (and track sales of over 13m).

Genre Focus – Dance

Album sales share: 4.9% (5th)
Singles sales share: 13.8% (4th)

TOP 5 BEST SELLERS

1. **DAVID GUETTA**
   Nothing But The Beat
   Virgin

2. **EXAMPLE**
   Playing In The Shadows
   Ministry Of Sound

3. **VARIOUS ARTISTS**
   XX – Twenty Years
   Ministry Of Sound

4. **VARIOUS ARTISTS**
   Clubland 19
   UMTV

5. **VARIOUS ARTISTS**
   Clubland 20
   UMTV

Source: Official Charts Company

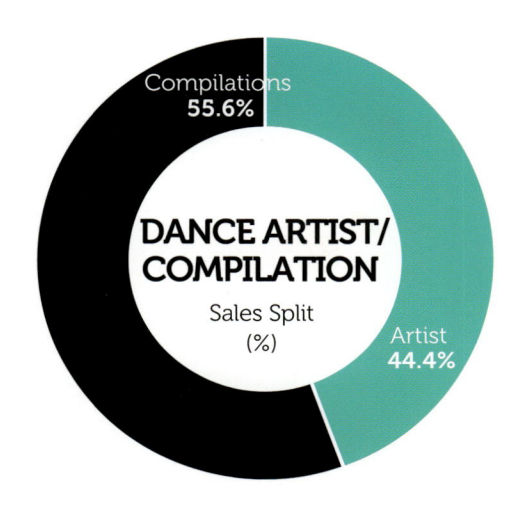

Dance's share of album sales slipped to below 5% in 2011, although it achieved a four-year high in the singles sector. There were plenty of successes in the latter to speak of, with almost a fifth (19) of the top 100 tracks of the year classified as Dance. LMFAO's **Party Rock Anthem** and Rihanna's **We Found Love** (co-credited to Calvin Harris) both made the year-end top five, having each spent several weeks at the top of the chart, and there were also number ones for **Example**, **DJ Fresh**, **Sak Noel** and **Nero**. As noted on page 17, one of the defining features of the singles year was the collaboration of artists from the Dance and Urban spheres, with **Chris Brown**, **Busta Rhymes** and **Kelly Rowland** among the many artists to have Dance-flavoured hits. Again the artist to marry these styles the most prolifically was **David Guetta**, whose hits included guest spots from R&B and Hip Hop luminaries such as **Flo Rida**, **Nicki Minaj**, **Usher**, **Taio Cruz** and **Ludacris**.

It was also **Guetta** who had the biggest success in the Dance albums market, his **Nothing But The Beat** album one of only two titles from the genre (along with **Example**'s *Playing In The Shadows*) to sell over a quarter of a million copies in 2011. Compilations remain a huge part of the Dance sector, accounting for over half of sales – Ministry's *XX – Twenty Years* anthology was the biggest seller, with two **Clubland** titles (see page 46) taking the next two places.

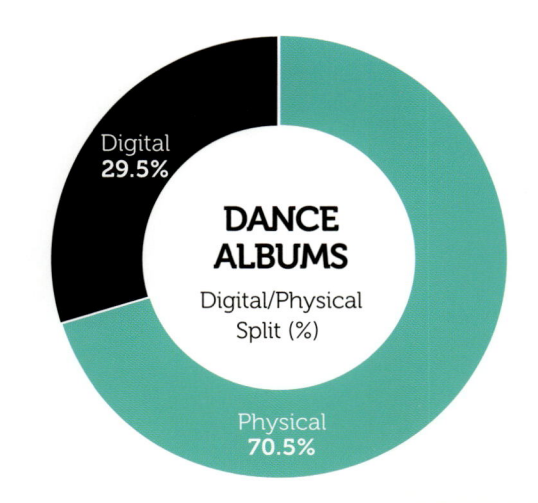

DANCE ARTIST/COMPILATION Sales Split (%)
- Compilations: 55.6%
- Artist: 44.4%

DANCE ALBUMS Digital/Physical Split (%)
- Digital: 29.5%
- Physical: 70.5%

Genre Focus – MOR/Easy

Album sales share: 7.9% (4th)
Singles sales share: 1.4% (6th)

As in 2011 **Michael Bublé** took the top spot in the MOR/Easy Listening genre chart, although this time round it was with his new **Christmas** album, released towards the end of October. The Canadian singer had another hugely successful year, his **Crazy Love** album – released in 2010 – still in great demand and his catalogue cumulatively accruing sales of well over 1.8m. **Susan Boyle**'s third album **Someone To Watch Over Me** rounded out the top three for the year, topping the chart on its week of release in November.

There were 11 MOR titles in the top 100 for the year, with two albums by **Alfie Boe** charting in the top 50. Released less than a year apart, **Bring Him Home** and **Alfie** both sold a quarter of a million copies, marking 2011 out to be a standout year for the tenor (see sidebar). There was also success for **Joe McElderry**, whose first album for Decca was a number two hit and whose **Classic Christmas** album was the 12th biggest MOR seller.

TOP 5 BEST SELLERS

1. **MICHAEL BUBLÉ**
   Christmas
   Warner Bros

2. **MICHAEL BUBLÉ**
   Crazy Love
   Warner Bros

3. **SUSAN BOYLE**
   Someone To Watch Over Me
   RCA Label Group

4. **RUMER**
   Seasons Of My Soul
   Atlantic Records UK

5. **ALFIE BOE**
   Bring Him Home
   Decca

Source: Official Charts Company

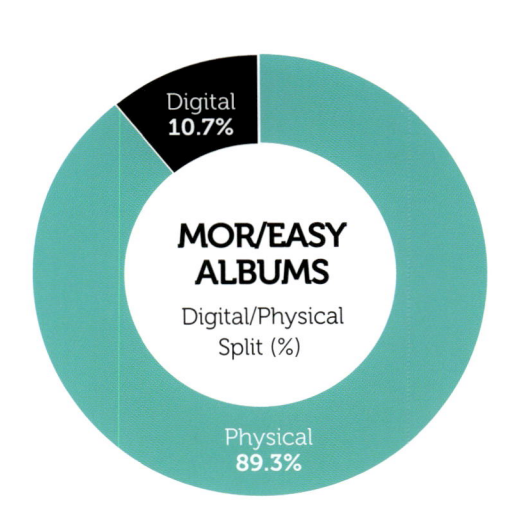

MOR/EASY ARTIST/COMPILATION Sales Split (%)
- Compilations 13.0%
- Artist 87.0%

MOR/EASY ALBUMS Digital/Physical Split (%)
- Digital 10.7%
- Physical 89.3%

PROFILE:
Alfie Boe's *Bring Him Home* and *Alfie*

It was an incredibly successful year for the tenor Alfie Boe, who had two albums chart in the year-end top 50, both selling a quarter of a million copies.

"We released *Bring Him Home* at the very end of 2010" says **Alex Cowan, Marketing Manager at Decca**. "Alfie had performed at the 25th anniversary *Les Misérables* concert in October and was invited to sing at the Royal Variety Show five days before Christmas, so it really capitalised on the huge reaction from that over the turn of the year, which is generally quite a fallow retail period. Off the back of its success we were able to build a database of Alfie's fans and ask them how they'd discovered him, where they bought the album, which tracks resonated the most and so on – that all fed into the plan for the next album.

WE ALSO MADE A CONSCIOUS DECISION TO HAVE MORE DIVERSE REPERTOIRE ON ALFIE, AND IT SEEMED TO PAY OFF – IT SOLD 250,000 COPIES IN NINE WEEKS.

We were also able to look at online data – both retail and streaming – and that helped us select tracks with which to promote *Alfie*, which came out in October 2011. By then he was nearing the end of his run of appearances in *Les Miserables,* and we were able to get him TV appearances on shows such as Titchmarsh, BBC Breakfast and Strictly, which gave him great exposure. He also did a Songs of Praise special, which really drove up pre-orders, and he performed on QVC too. We also made a conscious decision to have more diverse repertoire on *Alfie*, and it seemed to pay off – it sold 250,000 copies in nine weeks."

PROFILE:
hyperion

The independent label Hyperion celebrated its 30th anniversary in 2010 and claimed an improved 1.8% of the Classical albums market in 2011.

" The market has been tough" says **Sales and Marketing Manager Mike Spring**, "but highlights for us have included our two Stephen Hough titles, which were recordings of Chopin waltzes and Grieg/Liszt piano concertos. It was the bicentenary of Liszt's birth in 2011 and our Hamelin release and the box set of his complete piano works were also very popular – the latter sold over five and a half thousand copies: not bad for a 99-CD set! We also won a Gramophone award for our Finley/Drake Benjamin Britten CD. The next year's schedule is already filling out nicely, with quite a few key releases slated for autumn.

Digital is becoming increasingly important for us – it accounts for 13% of our turnover now. We launched our own download service two years ago and as a result we've really been able to tailor and hone our offer.

✶ DIGITAL IS BECOMING INCREASINGLY IMPORTANT FOR US – IT ACCOUNTS FOR 13% OF OUR TURNOVER NOW. ✶

The classical consumer puts an emphasis on sound quality, so we offer MP3 VBR, FLAC and ALAC downloads and find the lossless formats easily outsell MP3; we will go on to offer studio master quality in the near future. We've yet to see any real value in the streaming market, although clearly this is becoming an important way for people to sample music. We're trying different ways to reach out to customers but one of the big worries for us is the impact that the closure of bricks and mortar outlets has. Although the majority of our physical sales are online, shops put music in front of buyers and not all those high street customers are going to migrate over to buying on the internet. "

The Classical Market
Overall sales down but digital's share of sales up to 12.9%

Following a year when sales stabilised in 2010, there was a double digit drop (of 11%) in the sales of Classical music in 2011 as the market fell to 3.4m units.

Although change in formats and the pattern of retail sales should be taken into consideration, most of this decline can be attributed to sales of the best sellers. In 2010 the top two titles of the year sold more than 700,000 copies compared to 373,000 in 2011. The difference between the two figures represented the majority of the overall market decline of 423,000 lost sales.

The rate of growth in sales of digital Classical albums was an impressive 50%, well ahead of the total market increase but the volume increase was sufficient to offset only a quarter of the downturn in Classical CD sales, which fell by more than 16%.

Digital's share of Classical sales is still failing to match that in the broader album market but progress is being made – digital now accounts for 12.9% of sales, and on the most-downloaded title (**Ludovico Einaudi's *Islands***) physical took a minority share.

Mid price titles became more important to the market in 2011, rising to take a share of more than 20% and overtaking the budget sector in the process. Compilations also grew in significance, claiming 16.3% of sales compared with 13.8% in 2010.

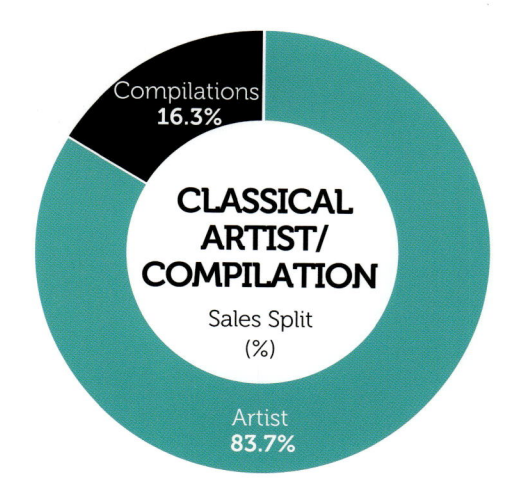

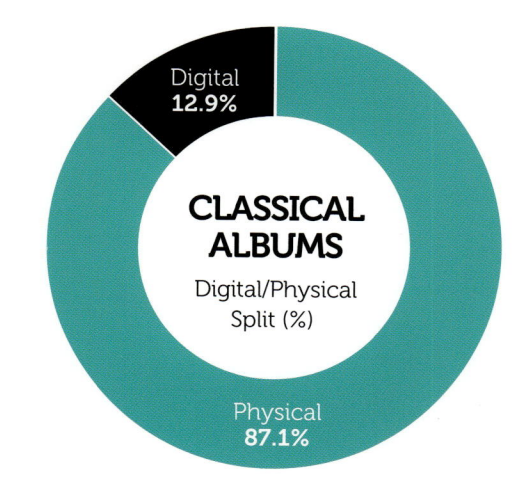

Classical Sales and Market Share

	Sales (m)	Market Share
2004	5.421	3.4%
2005	5.089	3.3%
2006	5.155	3.4%
2007	4.721	3.6%
2008	4.689	3.7%
2009	3.864	3.2%
2010	3.828	3.5%
2011	3.415	3.3%

Source: Official Charts Company

Digital's Share of Classical Album Sales
(% units)

2006	1.1%
2007	2.6%
2008	3.8%
2009	6.3%
2010	7.7%
2011	12.9%

Source: Official Charts Company

CLASSICAL ARTIST/ COMPILATION Sales Split (%)
- Compilations 16.3%
- Artist 83.7%

CLASSICAL ALBUMS Digital/Physical Split (%)
- Digital 12.9%
- Physical 87.1%

Best Sellers and Market Share – Classical

Clean sweep for Decca in the year-end chart

The chart for the best selling albums of the year was dominated by **Decca** releases, which accounted for all of the top 10 (including one joint venture with EMI) and 17 of the top 20. Sales of **Andre Rieu** albums topped 485,000 in 2011, and the Dutch violinist and conductor took the number one spot for the second year in a row (this time with **And The Waltz Goes On**), and he remained the best selling Classical artist overall. **Andrea Bocelli**'s **Concerto** was one of three Classical titles to feature in the year-end overall top 100, the third being **Now That's What I Call Classical** which recorded an impressive total of in excess of 135,000 copies, more than twice that of the best selling compilation in 2010.

Universal once again claimed well over half of sales in the market, although their share dipped slightly from 2010's 60.4%. EMI recorded a fairly sharp increase thanks in part to their share of sales of the **Now** compilation and it was also a good year for HNH, Hyperion, Delta, Chandos and LSO who all saw their market shares improve.

Classical Market Share by Record Company (% units)

	2006	2007	2008	2009	2010	2011
Universal Music	50.4	47.9	54.6	58.0	60.4	56.4
EMI Music	16.4	16.3	11.4	9.2	8.4	13.4
Sony Music	9.7	8.9	12.6	11.9	10.3	6.2
HNH	10.0	9.0	7.3	7.2	5.8	6.1
Warner Music	2.6	1.9	1.3	1.8	2.2	3.0
Hyperion	1.1	1.2	1.2	1.5	1.5	1.8
Delta	0.1	-	0.1	0.1	0.2	1.2
Chandos	0.4	0.6	0.7	0.9	0.9	1.1
LSO	0.6	0.6	0.6	0.6	0.6	1.0
Union Square Music	1.0	0.8	1.2	1.5	1.4	0.9
X5	-	-	-	-	0.3	0.9
Harmonia Mundi	0.5	0.6	0.6	0.8	0.9	0.8
Demon Music Group	2.7	4.7	3.0	1.6	1.6	0.7
Coro	-	0.1	0.2	0.3	0.4	0.6
T2 Entertainment	-	-	-	-	0.2	0.5
ECM	0.2	0.2	0.2	0.3	0.5	0.4
Collegium	0.2	0.2	0.4	0.3	0.3	0.3
Foreign Media Group	-	-	-	0.1	0.1	0.3

Source: Official Charts Company

TOP 10 CLASSICAL ALBUMS 2011

1. **ANDRE RIEU & JOHANN STRAUSS ORCHESTRA**
   And The Waltz Goes On
   Decca

2. **ANDREA BOCELLI**
   Concerto – One Night In Central Park
   Decca

3. **VARIOUS ARTISTS**
   Now That's What I Call Classical
   Decca/EMI TV

4. **ANDRE RIEU & JOHANN STRAUSS ORCHESTRA**
   Moonlight Serenade
   Decca

5. **BAND OF HM ROYAL MARINES**
   Summon The Heroes
   Decca

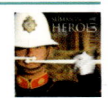

6. **KATHERINE JENKINS**
   One Fine Day
   Decca

7. **MILOS KARADAGLIC**
   The Guitar
   Decca

8. **HAYLEY WESTENRA/ENNIO MORRICONE**
   Paradiso
   Decca

9. **ANDRE RIEU**
   Forever Vienna
   Decca

10. **BAND OF THE COLDSTREAM GUARDS**
    Pride Of The Nation
    Decca

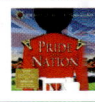

Source: Official Charts Company

Sales by Chart Position – Albums

Adele helps push average weekly top spot sales above 100k

Adele's *21* was at number one for 10 of the first 13 weeks of the year, which explains the extraordinarily high average weekly sale for that position in the first quarter. In week 13 it sold over a quarter of a million copies and never dipped below 130,000, hence the average of 148,875 – almost three times that reported for Q1 2010. The album's success also had some bearing on the second quarter average of 90,525, although big sellers from **Foo Fighters** and **Lady Gaga** also helped bring the figure up from 54,375 in 2010. Number one sales in Q3 were slightly up on 2010's but Q4's average was some way short of a year earlier.

There were sales falls across almost every chart position, with only the titles towards the top of the chart each week selling more copies than a year previously. The outstanding performance of *21* is thrown into relief in the second table – whereas in the previous five years the year's biggest seller had failed to account for more than 1.5% of the entire market, in 2011 it easily topped 3%. Its dominance ensured that the top 100 sellers cumulatively represented close to a third of all albums sold in 2011.

Average Weekly Album Sales by Chart Position

Chart position	1	5	10	20	30	40	50	75
2002	97,775	33,200	23,900	15,500	11,250	8,225	6,450	3,650
2003	88,425	39,800	25,800	16,750	11,850	8,750	6,825	4,000
2004	92,400	39,875	27,525	17,125	12,175	9,050	6,825	3,975
2005	116,850	42,575	28,175	18,400	12,850	9,175	7,200	4,150
2006	119,775	38,175	26,675	16,450	11,325	8,625	6,475	3,875
2007	93,775	30,225	20,725	13,475	9,775	7,375	5,400	3,150
2008	101,175	30,775	20,200	12,400	8,900	6,775	5,125	3,100
2009	93,850	31,975	21,725	12,825	8,700	6,600	5,175	3,200
2010	87,525	28,075	18,925	11,500	7,950	5,775	4,575	2,975
2011	109,175	30,475	18,325	10,150	7,025	5,275	4,075	2,550
2011 Q1	148,875	27,075	16,375	8,950	6,050	4,525	3,500	2,300
2011 Q2	90,525	19,975	12,000	7,000	5,075	3,975	3,100	2,000
2011 Q3	59,175	19,050	10,425	6,500	4,575	3,550	2,900	1,875
2011 Q4	138,125	55,825	34,550	18,175	12,350	9,025	6,800	4,000

Source: Millward Brown/Official Charts Company

Top Sellers as a Percentage of Total Albums Market (%)

	2006	2007	2008	2009	2010	2011
Annual Best Seller	1.0	1.1	1.3	1.3	1.5	3.3
Top 10	6.9	7.2	8.2	8.4	8.4	11.4
Top 40	18.6	17.1	18.1	20.0	19.8	22.9
Top 75	27.1	24.8	25.2	27.4	26.8	29.6
Top 100	31.4	28.8	29.0	31.2	30.4	32.9

Source: BPI based on Official Charts Company data

Sales by Chart Position – Singles

Sales increase in every top 75 chart position in 2011

The average number of copies sold to get to number one on the weekly singles chart rose to its highest level in nine years in 2011. There were increases in every position measured in the top 75, with almost 30,000 now the average sales for a single in the chart at number 10.

Although the weekly total for a number one in the first quarter was down on 2010, it rose in Q2 to over 80,000 (from 74,300 a year earlier) thanks to big sellers from **Jennifer Lopez**, **LMFAO**, **Pitbull** and **Example**, whose **Changed The Way You Kissed Me** sold over 115,000 copies in its week of release in June. The figure for a number one in Q3 was also up on 2010's, with particularly strong sales achieved by **DJ Fresh**, **The Wanted** and **Olly Murs**. **One Direction**'s debut single **What Makes You Beautiful** was the fastest seller of the quarter, however, selling almost 154,000 in its first week. Despite the release of the **Military Wives** single in December, Q4 number ones in 2011 sold slightly less on average than they did a year earlier.

Adele's **Someone Like You** accounted for 0.7% of all singles sold, the highest share in three years, with the top 100 best sellers responsible for 23.7% of the total.

Average Weekly Singles Sales by Chart Position

Chart position	1	5	10	20	30	40	50	75
2002	144,300	31,975	18,425	9,050	5,450	3,400	2,250	1,250
2003	70,175	23,050	13,300	6,525	3,850	2,550	1,725	725
2004	71,400	18,900	10,875	5,550	3,350	2,125	1,400	550
2005	82,450	17,300	10,375	5,350	3,375	2,350	1,625	800
2006	55,975	17,725	11,125	6,475	4,200	2,975	2,225	1,250
2007	55,350	17,875	11,325	6,450	4,500	3,400	2,675	1,700
2008	71,550	23,275	15,050	8,400	5,650	4,150	3,275	2,125
2009	92,900	34,575	22,350	12,375	8,625	6,425	4,975	3,025
2010	102,200	42,850	28,075	14,875	10,075	7,100	5,375	3,225
2011	103,325	42,950	29,225	16,250	11,175	8,100	6,200	3,750
2011 Q1	102,675	41,850	27,450	15,475	10,875	7,950	6,100	3,800
2011 Q2	80,800	43,000	28,750	16,625	11,425	8,075	6,050	3,700
2011 Q3	93,575	41,925	28,250	16,050	10,950	7,975	5,925	3,475
2011 Q4	136,250	45,075	32,500	16,825	11,400	8,410	6,700	4,075

Source: Millward Brown/Official Charts Company

Top Sellers as a Percentage of Total Singles Market (%)

	2006	2007	2008	2009	2010	2011
Annual Best Seller	1.2	0.9	0.8	0.6	0.5	0.7
Top 10	6.1	4.9	4.6	4.6	4.4	5.2
Top 40	13.9	12.4	12.2	12.8	12.8	13.8
Top 75	20.0	17.5	17.6	19.0	19.7	20.2
Top 100	23.1	20.1	20.2	22.3	23.4	23.7

Source: BPI based on Official Charts Company data

Example

Best Selling Albums – Sales Analysis

Five titles pass 1m sales tally in 2011

While the number of top selling titles has held up in recent years – since 2008 at least 10 albums in every year have sold over 750,000 copies – there has been a decrease in the total selling over 100k in each year since 2004. In that year 256 albums sold over this level (including 13 that sold over half a million copies) but this has decreased to 140 in 2011.

The majority of this loss has come in the 100-249k sales bracket: in 2003 178 titles sold between these two markers but only 91 did in 2011, the first time this century that the total has dipped below 100.

While the titles by **Adele** this year and **Take That's** *Progress* in 2010 have shown that there are still albums capable of extraordinary success, the obvious conclusion would seem to be that fewer customers are motivated to make mainstream purchases outside of these 'blockbuster' releases.

While a great number of albums – almost 339,000 – sold at least one copy in 2011, the vast majority are classed in the very lowest sales brackets. Over 97% sold fewer than 1,000 copies, with almost 300,000 selling less than 100 according to Millward Brown's sales data.

Number of Albums Sold by Sales Threshold

Sales	No. of Titles
100,000+	140
10,000-99,999	1,244
1,000-9,999	7,588
101-999	31,487
1-100	298,504
Total	338,963

Source: BPI based on Official Charts Company/Millward Brown data

Number of Albums Sold by Sales Threshold (100,000 sales or more)

	100,000-249,999	250,000-499,999	500,000-749,999	750,000-999,999	1m+	Total 100k+
2002	141	48	18	7	6	220
2003	178	39	19	10	7	253
2004	174	43	19	13	7	256
2005	138	55	14	13	8	228
2006	129	56	19	9	6	219
2007	118	54	12	1	5	190
2008	154	43	9	4	6	216
2009	132	38	12	6	6	194
2010	110	33	9	6	4	162
2011	91	33	5	6	5	140

Source: BPI based on Official Charts Company data

Best Selling Singles – Sales Analysis

Two titles sell 1m for first time in 9 years

The continued growth in the singles market is reflected in the sales accrued by the most successful titles of the year – two passed the million sales mark for the first time since 2002, when the debut singles by **Will Young** and **Gareth Gates** were released, although 2004 did see the release of one million seller (by **Band Aid 20**). More singles than at any time this century are passing the half a million mark too – 23 did so in 2011, a significant improvement on the previous year's tally of 18. In total, 188 singles sold more than 100,000, the highest total yet and almost five times that recorded in 2005, when digital services were still in their early stages.

More than a million tracks sold at least one copy in 2011 – up significantly on the 878,500 that did so in 2010. As in the albums market, the bulk recorded fewer than 1,000 sales (98.5%) with, according to Millward Brown's data, around 70% of tracks selling less than 10 copies. The top 5,000 sellers were responsible for two thirds of all singles sold.

Number of Singles Sold by Sales Threshold

Sales	No. of Titles
100,000+	188
10,000-99,999	1,877
1,000-9,999	12,784
101-999	57,410
1-100	937,791
Total	1,010,050

Source: BPI based on Official Charts Company/Millward Brown data

Number of Singles Sold by Sales Threshold (100,000 sales or more)

	100,000-249,999	250,000-499,999	500,000-749,999	750,000-999,999	1m+	Total 100k+
2002	88	28	5	2	2	125
2003	44	15	2	-	-	61
2004	36	7	1	-	1	45
2005	25	11	1	1	-	38
2006	61	6	1	1	-	69
2007	59	18	1	1	-	79
2008	71	27	1	2	-	101
2009	105	53	9	3	-	170
2010	102	65	15	3	-	185
2011	106	59	13	8	2	188

Source: BPI based on Official Charts Company data

Monthly and Daily Sales Patterns – Albums
Saturday still key for album shopping

The release of two of the best selling albums of the year – Bruno Mars' *Doo-Wops & Hooligans* and Adele's *21* – in weeks three and four respectively ensured that January accounted for its largest share of annual sales since the turn of the century. **Adele**'s album was a particularly strong seller in what is often a quiet period of the year, selling over 208,000 copies in its week of release. Sales in March were also relatively strong, again mainly as a result of *21*'s extraordinary performance but also due to the release of the debut album from **Jessie J**, which sold over 105,000 copies in its first week.

The share of sales taking place in June was also up, with the albums by **Lady Gaga** and **Adele** selling almost 460,000 copies between them. The final month of the year was also relatively strong, **Michael Bublé**'s *Christmas* and *Now 80* faring particularly well over the festive period.

The importance of Saturday in terms of physical album shopping has ensured that it remains the busiest day of the week, although its share has been diminishing for some years and Sunday actually claims the largest share (16.8%) in the digital market.

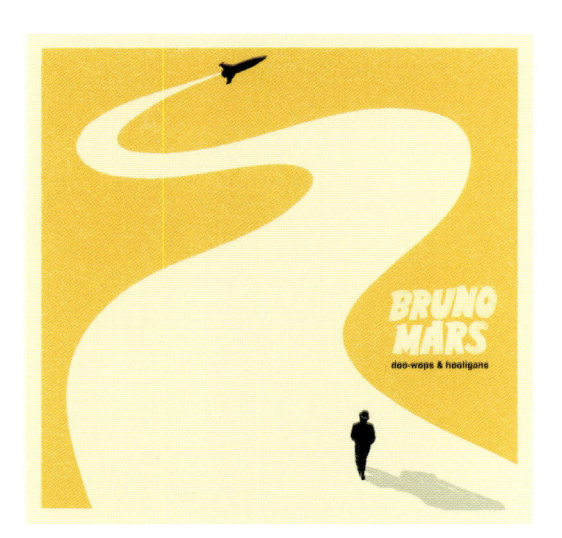

Monthly Sales Patterns – Albums (% of annual total units)

	2004	2005	2006	2007	2008	2009	2010	2011
January	6.6	6.4	6.7	7.1	6.7	7.2	6.8	7.4
February	6.5	6.6	6.6	7.6	6.7	6.3	7.3	7.3
March	8.5	9.0	8.7	8.7	8.9	8.1	9.0	9.1
April	6.5	5.6	6.6	6.4	6.1	6.0	5.8	6.2
May	5.6	5.4	5.8	6.1	5.6	5.7	6.1	6.1
June	7.6	9.0	8.0	8.3	8.6	7.6	8.1	8.6
July	6.6	6.8	6.4	6.5	6.3	6.6	6.8	5.9
August	6.1	6.1	6.3	5.9	6.0	5.6	6.3	5.8
September	7.4	8.1	8.0	7.7	7.7	7.5	7.5	7.5
October	6.7	6.5	6.6	6.2	6.5	6.2	6.3	6.3
November	8.2	8.8	8.5	8.5	8.2	8.6	9.9	9.1
December	23.6	21.7	21.7	21.1	22.7	24.5	20.2	20.7

Source: BPI based on Official Charts Company data
Note: March, June, September and December are five week months; December 2004 and 2009 were six week months

Album Sales by Day of Week (% down)

	2007	2008	2009	2010	2011
Sunday	10.4	10.3	10.6	10.6	11.0
Monday	14.8	15.1	15.5	15.9	16.3
Tuesday	12.9	13.5	13.9	13.7	13.8
Wednesday	12.5	13.2	13.4	13.2	13.1
Thursday	13.4	12.9	13.5	13.7	13.6
Friday	15.5	15.1	14.6	15.3	15.0
Saturday	20.5	20.0	18.5	17.5	17.2

Source: Millward Brown/Official Charts Company

Monthly and Daily Sales Patterns – Singles
Sunday still busiest day in singles market

Every month in the second quarter of 2011 accounted for a greater share of singles sales than it had done in the previous year. Tracks by **Bruno Mars**, **Pitbull** and **LMFAO** all sold over 200,000 copies in May, helping its share up to 7.7%, while June's 9.5% was driven by an exceptional performance for a second consecutive month of **Pitbull**'s *Give Me Everything* which, along with **Example**'s *Changed The Way You Kissed Me*, sold over 300,000 copies across the month's five weeks.

September saw big selling new singles released by **One Direction** and **Pixie Lott** although **Maroon 5**'s *Moves Like Jagger* was the big hit of the month, selling over 376,000 copies. Sales in December represented an unusually low share of the annual total – 11.3% – even though 5.8m singles were sold in the last week of the year.

Sunday remains the busiest shopping day of the week in the singles market, although in the declining physical market Monday is still key, with almost 30% of all purchases taking place then. Across the entire singles market the weekend accounts for over a third of all sales.

Monthly Sales Patterns – Singles (% of annual total units)

	2004	2005	2006	2007	2008	2009	2010	2011
January	6.8	5.1	6.5	7.3	7.6	8.2	8.4	8.0
February	7.1	6.1	6.9	7.4	7.3	7.6	8.2	7.8
March	11.4	10.3	8.8	9.4	9.3	9.4	9.3	9.3
April	8.5	6.6	8.2	7.0	7.0	7.2	6.9	7.2
May	7.5	7.5	7.5	7.0	6.9	7.5	7.2	7.7
June	8.9	8.9	9.3	9.0	8.8	8.9	9.2	9.5
July	7.0	6.9	7.3	7.2	7.2	7.4	7.6	7.5
August	6.3	7.0	7.3	7.1	7.0	6.8	7.0	7.1
September	8.9	10.0	9.8	8.9	9.1	8.6	8.7	9.3
October	6.5	8.4	8.0	8.2	8.0	7.3	7.4	7.7
November	7.8	8.7	8.5	8.6	8.7	7.7	8.0	7.6
December	13.3	14.5	12.0	12.8	13.1	13.3	12.0	11.3

Source: BPI based on Official Charts Company data
Note: March, June, September and December are five week months; December 2004 and 2009 were six week months

Singles Sales by Day of Week (% down)

	2007	2008	2009	2010	2011
Sunday	16.5	17.1	17.5	17.9	17.9
Monday	14.6	13.8	14.2	14.2	13.9
Tuesday	13.5	12.7	13.2	13.0	12.8
Wednesday	12.9	12.3	12.8	12.6	12.6
Thursday	13.0	13.1	12.9	12.7	13.0
Friday	13.6	14.1	13.7	13.6	13.8
Saturday	15.9	16.9	15.8	16.1	16.0

Source: Millward Brown/Official Charts Company

SALES METRICS

Sales by Region – Albums and Singles
London accounts for a fifth of album sales

Sales made in the London region again accounted for over 20% of all albums bought in 2011, and it was one of seven to take a larger percentage of sales than its national population share. The size of the region meant that it took the biggest slice of sales in every genre, although MOR (18.0%) and Country (18.1%) comparatively fared the worst, with Londoners 'outscoring' most heavily on Jazz (25.1%), Classical (23.3%) and Urban (22.8%). Buyers in the region took a larger share of sales within the artist albums market than they did on compilations and were responsible for a quarter of all digital albums bought across the year. Londoners also overbought relative to their population size in the largely digital singles market, taking a 23.6% share.

Music consumers in the South and South East were also among the most proportionally active – the region represents 8.8% of the UK population but 11.0% of all albums sold in 2011 were bought there. Their purchasing of digital albums and singles was also relatively high.

Some regional genre patterns emerge upon closer inspection of the data. Country and Folk score especially well in Scotland, as does the former in Northern Ireland, while the North East's largest share of album sales occurs in the MOR market. The East region, interestingly, overbuys on every single genre, with Urban particularly popular.

Regional Sales by Genre and Format 2011 (% across)

	London	South & South East	South West	Wales & West	Midlands	East	Yorkshire	North East	North West	Border	Scotland	Northern Ireland
Total Market – Albums	20.4	11.0	3.1	8.3	14.1	8.6	8.0	4.3	10.1	1.1	8.7	2.4
Rock	20.3	10.8	3.0	8.1	13.9	8.1	8.1	4.3	10.1	1.1	9.8	2.3
Pop	18.6	11.0	3.2	8.6	14.3	8.8	8.5	4.5	10.4	1.1	8.4	2.6
Urban	22.8	11.2	3.0	8.2	14.5	9.2	7.5	3.8	10.3	0.9	6.6	2.0
MOR/Easy Listening	18.0	10.7	3.2	8.8	14.4	8.4	8.4	5.0	10.5	1.1	8.9	2.6
Dance	21.2	11.3	3.1	8.0	13.7	8.5	7.6	4.4	9.9	1.2	8.8	2.4
Classical	23.3	11.9	3.4	8.3	14.6	8.5	7.0	3.9	8.9	1.0	7.2	2.0
Jazz	25.1	12.2	3.3	7.8	13.7	8.6	6.7	3.6	9.0	0.8	7.4	1.8
Country	18.1	10.6	3.2	8.1	13.0	8.2	7.5	4.3	9.4	1.2	11.6	4.9
Folk	19.2	10.6	3.6	8.1	13.5	8.1	7.6	4.3	9.4	1.1	11.6	2.9
Artist Albums	20.7	11.0	3.1	8.2	14.0	8.5	8.0	4.3	10.1	1.1	8.7	2.4
Compilations	19.1	11.1	3.3	8.8	14.6	9.0	8.1	4.3	10.0	1.1	8.2	2.4
Digital Albums	25.0	12.0	3.2	7.9	12.8	9.3	6.4	3.9	8.0	1.2	8.1	2.1
All Singles	23.6	11.7	3.2	8.2	12.7	9.3	6.4	4.2	8.0	1.4	8.7	2.5
% Population Split	19.9	8.8	3.0	7.8	16.0	6.9	9.6	4.7	11.4	1.0	8.0	2.9

Source: Official Charts Company/ISBA
Note: some repercentaging owing to regionally unattributable digital data

Sales by Format Variant

Multi-disc sets account for a quarter of physical album sales

Some 86.6m albums were sold on physical formats in 2011, encompassing CD, vinyl and a small number of relatively minor other product types. Every version of each physical release on the Official Charts Company database is assigned a variant code which designates whether a particular edition is being sold as a single or multiple disc as well as denoting packaging variations. Some releases will be available with multiple variants.

The main table lists out the share of sales attributable to each album variant. Standard CDs accounted for over two thirds of physical album sales – these are most often the single disc 'main editions' of artist albums. 'Two Packs' were responsible for a 14.8% share in 2011 and are most commonly associated with compilations such as the *Now* series, although extra-disc repackages of artist albums (such as Take That's *Progressed*) can also fall into this category. Three-disc sets represented around one in 15 physical album sales, with compilations such as *Now That's What I Call Disney* particularly big sellers, while examples of Bonus DVD releases included both artist titles (such as Michael Bublé's *Christmas*) and compilations such as *Pop Party 9*.

Vinyl represented 0.4% of physical album sales and standard versions in this market amounted to just over half (51.9%) of the market, with doubles representing a significant 30% share.

Physical Format Sales 2011 – Split by Variant

Variant	Sales	% of Sales
Standard	58,154,593	67.2%
2 Pack	12,806,220	14.8%
3 Pack	5,749,397	6.6%
Bonus DVD	2,791,820	3.2%
Remix	1,729,543	2.0%
Special Packaging	1,569,653	1.8%
5 Pack	1,026,009	1.2%
Enhanced CD	927,304	1.1%
4 Pack	872,195	1.0%
Vinyl	337,048	0.4%
Import	226,467	0.3%
6 Pack	109,340	0.1%
Greater than a 9 Pack	100,706	0.1%
Super Audio	72,054	0.1%
8 Pack	36,371	-
Box Set	33,034	-
7 Pack	14,261	-
9 Pack	11,366	-
True 3D	2,281	-
DualDisc	1,249	-
Total	**86,570,911**	**100%**

Source: BPI based on Official Charts Company/Millward Brown data

Vinyl Sales 2011 – Split by Variant

Variant	Sales	% of Sales
Standard	174,847	51.9%
2 Pack	101,255	30.0%
Special Packaging	23,014	6.8%
Coloured Vinyl	11,374	3.4%
3 Pack	9,068	2.7%
Import	4,607	1.4%
4 Pack	3,533	1.0%
10 Inch Vinyl	3,274	1.0%
Picture Disc	1,504	0.4%
5 Pack	1,433	0.4%
6 Pack	1,082	0.3%
Greater than a 9 Pack	846	0.3%
Box Set	453	0.1%
9 Pack	294	0.1%
8 Pack	182	0.1%
Remix	142	-
7 Pack	140	-
Total	**337,048**	**100%**

Source: BPI based on Official Charts Company/Millward Brown data

The Gift Market

One in four buys an album as a gift in 2011

The 'gifting' of physical albums is still of key importance to the music industry, with data from Kantar's Worldpanel survey showing that over a third (33.7%) of expenditure in this market is in the form of gifts, rising to over half (53%) in the final 12 weeks of the year. The same survey's data also shows, however, that the number of people buying CDs as a gift is falling – in 2011 just over a quarter (25.8%) of the UK population did so, down from 27.3% in 2010 and 29.3% the year before that. Over half (53.9%) of all music buyers are making gift purchases, but this is down from 63.2% two years previously. It should be noted, however, that Kantar's data only includes physical format gift expenditure and does not capture spend on digital gift cards.

One of the key factors seems to be that one of the most active music-buying groups – the 35 to 44 year olds – is reducing its spend on gifts quite significantly, its share now down to 21.0%. The youngest and oldest age groups are claiming a greater percentage of expenditure, but these both sit outside the four highest spending age groups in the physical albums market. The share attributable to women is also falling: whereas in 2009 they spent the most on gifts, now men do.

Music Gifting – Penetration* (%)

	2009	2010	2011
Total Population	29.3	27.3	25.8
All Music Buyers	63.2	63.1	53.9

Source: Kantar Worldpanel
Base: physical music
*percentage who have made at least one gift purchase

Music Gifting – Expenditure by Age (% down)

	2009	2010	2011
13-19	7.5	8.2	9.8
20-24	6.9	6.9	5.4
25-34	15.5	14.0	15.0
35-44	23.4	21.6	21.0
45-54	23.6	24.4	24.5
55-64	14.4	15.6	14.3
65-79	8.7	9.3	10.1
Total	**100**	**100**	**100**

Source: Kantar Worldpanel
Base: physical music

Music Gifting – Expenditure by Gender and Social Group (% down)

	2009	2010	2011
Female	52.6	48.8	48.1
Male	47.4	51.2	51.9
AB	19.0	17.2	18.4
C1	36.1	38.0	38.4
C2	25.6	24.3	22.5
DE	19.4	20.6	20.7

Source: Kantar Worldpanel
Base: physical music

54%
OVER HALF OF MUSIC BUYERS PURCHASED A CD AS A GIFT IN 2011

The Gift Market

Gifts account for over a third of physical album expenditure

Kantar's respondents are asked to classify each of their physical album purchases in one of three groups – bought as a gift for someone else, family use or personal use. While the share of expenditure gifting accounts for has fluctuated since 2009, family use has grown steadily, perhaps as a result of the squeeze on disposable income in that time. Compilations are more likely to be bought for this purpose than artist albums, of which the majority are bought for personal use; compilations are also more likely to be bought as a present than artist albums.

Heavy buyers (those spending over £67.20 in a year) account for the greatest share of spend in each purchase category, although they claim a much higher percentage on CDs bought for personal use. Light buyers (those spending less than £22.96) take their largest share in the gift market, where they represent almost a quarter of expenditure.

Reason for Purchase 2011 – Artist vs Compilation Albums

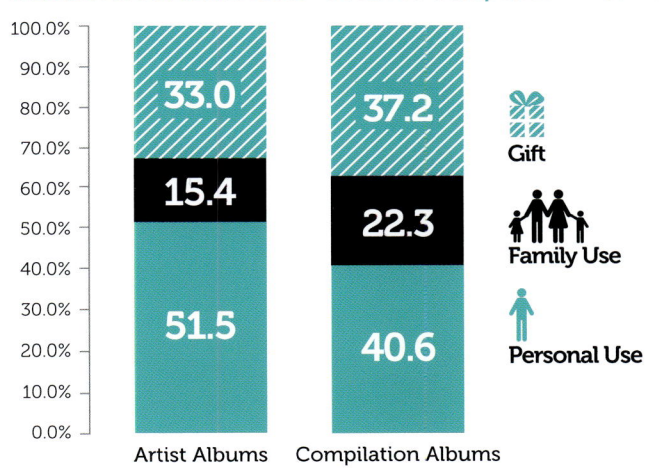

	Artist Albums	Compilation Albums
Gift	33.0	37.2
Family Use	15.4	22.3
Personal Use	51.5	40.6

Source: Kantar Worldpanel
Base: expenditure

Reason for Purchase – Physical Albums
(% down)

	2009	2010	2011
Personal Use	51.6	49.5	49.8
Family Use	14.0	15.7	16.5
Gift	34.4	34.8	33.7
Total	**100**	**100**	**100**

Source: Kantar Worldpanel
Base: expenditure

Purchase Type by Buyer Group 2011
(% across)

	Heavy	Medium	Light	Total
Total Market	52.5	30.5	16.9	100
Personal Use	60.6	26.2	13.2	100
Family Use	55.6	29.8	14.5	100
Gift	39.0	37.4	23.6	100

Source: Kantar Worldpanel
Base: physical music expenditure

PRICING

Retail Prices

Retail cost of CDs falls to new low

Tables in this book with the source given as Kantar Worldpanel are based on the purchasing trends of 15,000 demographically representative British individuals. The data presented in these tables are therefore based on consumer research rather than retail sales records.

With the exception of digital there were decreases across the board in the average cost to the consumer of albums in 2011. The price of a physical album – even when multi-disc releases and higher ticket items such as vinyl are factored in – is only £7.19, with a single-disc CD costing an average of £6.71, its lowest ever. When all formats, both physical and digital, are considered the average price drops to £7.02 as download albums retail for the relatively low average price of £6.43.

Compilations albums are often double or triple disc sets and this pushes their retail price to a level higher than that of artist releases – £7.88 compared to £7.07. Prices in both markets have fallen steadily however, with a drop of £1 over the last two years in the compilations market.

Kantar's respondents reported CD prices as being lowest at Chains and Multiples again in 2011, although it should be noted that this was across a relatively small sector carrying a limited range of titles. Albums bought via online retailers (such as Amazon and Play) cost an average of just over £7.

Average Retail Prices

	2009	2010	2011
Albums (incl. dig)	£7.65	£7.32	£7.02
Albums (excl. dig)	£7.88	£7.55	£7.19
Single CD Albums	£7.17	£6.93	£6.71
Double CD Albums	£9.85	£9.29	£8.72
Digital Albums	£5.86	£6.11	£6.43
Total Compilation Albums	£8.87	£8.66	£7.88
Artist Albums	£7.69	£7.35	£7.07

Source: Kantar Worldpanel

CD Albums – Sales by Price Group (% down)

	2009	2010	2011
Under £4	14.4	15.5	19.5
£4.00-£5.99	19.8	22.9	22.3
£6.00-£7.99	17.8	18.0	17.5
£8.00-£9.99	28.5	26.7	25.2
£10.00-£11.99	9.0	7.8	8.1
£12.00-£13.99	7.0	6.1	4.7
£14.00-£15.99	2.2	1.8	1.7
£16.00+	1.4	1.2	0.9
Total	**100**	**100**	**100**

Source: Kantar Worldpanel

Average Prices Paid for CD Albums by Type of Retailer

	2009	2010	2011	% change
Total	**£7.88**	**£7.55**	**£7.19**	**-4.8%**
Music Specialists	£8.13	£7.83	£7.54	-3.7%
Chains/Multiples	£6.52	£6.56	£6.32	-3.7%
Supermarkets	£8.21	£7.99	£7.59	-5.0%
Internet	£7.63	£7.17	£7.02	-2.1%

Source: Kantar Worldpanel

85%
PERCENTAGE OF ALBUMS BOUGHT FOR UNDER £10 IN 2011

Sales by Price Category – Albums

Budget and Mid Price sectors both record sales increases

Full price albums constituted less than two thirds of volume sales in 2011, decreasing from a 67.8% share to 64.9%. The sector's share has fluctuated in recent years but in 2004 was accounting for over three quarters of the market. Some 6.9m fewer albums were sold in this price group in 2011, equivalent to an 8.8% decrease – sales of full price compilations were down particularly steeply, dropping by 20.2%.

Sales improved in both the mid and budget sectors, although this was not enough to compensate for the losses experienced in the full price market. **Adele**'s first album *19* was one of the key drivers of the rise in the mid price market although albums by **Plan B**, **Lady Gaga** and **Michael Bublé** all sold well over a quarter of a million copies each. The budget price bracket is more geared towards compilation albums, which constituted 10 of the top 20 sellers, although artist collections by **Thin Lizzy** and **Dolly Parton** both featured in the top five.

MID PRICE TOP SELLERS 2011

1. **ADELE**
   19
   XL Recordings

2. **PLAN B**
   The Defamation Of Strickland Banks
   Atlantic Records UK

3. **LADY GAGA**
   The Fame
   Polydor

4. **MICHAEL BUBLÉ**
   Crazy Love
   Warner Bros

5. **AMY WINEHOUSE**
   Back To Black
   Universal Island

Source: Official Charts Company

BUDGET TOP SELLERS 2011

1. **VARIOUS ARTISTS**
   The Ultimate Family Christmas
   Go Entertain

2. **THIN LIZZY**
   Waiting For An Alibi – The Collection
   Spectrum Music

3. **DOLLY PARTON**
   Ultimate
   RCA Label Group

4. **VARIOUS ARTISTS**
   It's Christmas
   Big 3

5. **VARIOUS ARTISTS**
   Ultimate Dance
   Demon Music

Source: Official Charts Company

Price Category 2011 Sales Split (%)

- Budget 9.3%
- Mid Price 25.8%
- Full Price 64.9%

Album Sales by Price Category (units thousands)

	2008	2009	2010	2011	% change
Budget	14,791	9,807	9,603	10,223	+6.5%
Mid Price	26,287	24,663	27,571	28,413	+3.1%
Full Price	90,250	91,132	78,407	71,522	-8.8%

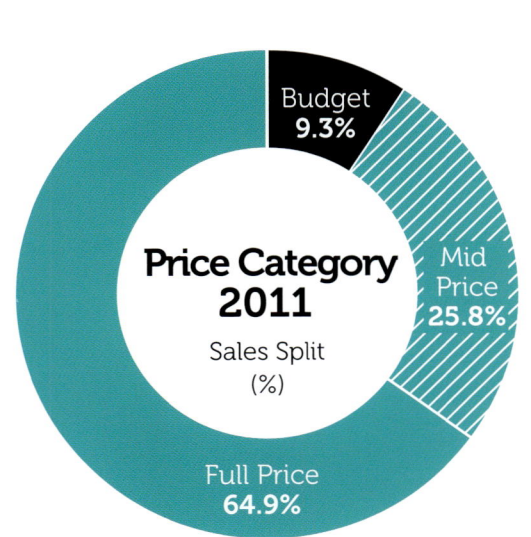

Source: Official Charts Company

PROFILE:
The Vaccines' *What Did You Expect From The Vaccines?*

IN A YEAR THAT WAS NOTICEABLY SHORT ON ROCK BREAKTHROUGHS THE VACCINES BUCKED THAT TREND WITH THEIR DEBUT ALBUM, WHICH WAS THE SECOND-BIGGEST SELLING ROCK DEBUT OF THE YEAR.

Formed in early 2010, the band's demo of their song *If You Wanna* caught the attention of a number of tastemakers in August of that year, including Radio 1's Zane Lowe who made it his 'Hottest Record in the World'. After a number of acclaimed live performances The Vaccines' first single *Wreckin' Bar* (*Ra Ra Ra*) was released in a limited run of 1,000 copies. The ensuing positive reaction saw the band record a session for 6Music and also appear on Later With Jools Holland. At the end of the year they featured in a number of 'tipped' lists, including the BBC's Sound Of 2011 and the shortlist for the BRIT Awards Critics' Choice.

The band's first release for Columbia, the *Post Break-Up Sex* single, was released in January and broke the top 40, while a slot on the NME Awards tour helped keep their profile high. After a trip to SXSW the band's debut *What Did You Expect From The Vaccines?* was released, breaking the top five in the second week of March. The festival season brought appearances at Reading/Leeds and Glastonbury, also inspiring the band to crowd-source photos of their fans for the video to their single *Wetsuit*, which has now been viewed closed to 1.5m times. In total four singles were released from the album and its appearance in a number of end-of-year polls gave it a fresh boost at the start of 2012, when it returned to the top 10 for three weeks. At the time of writing (April 2012) it has sold over 300,000 copies.

Breakthrough Analysis
Number of breakthroughs steady in 2011

The criterion for inclusion in this analysis of 'breakthrough' artists is those who have sold 100,000 copies of an album for the first time in the UK in a five-year period, so the 2011 analysis relates to albums released between 2007-2011. Consequently some slower-selling titles may have been excluded. Soundtrack albums and cast recordings are not included in the analysis.

Although the overall number of breakthroughs made in 2011 was only marginally ahead of the 2010 total, there was an increase in the number of UK acts passing the 100,000 sales threshold for the first time, from 18 to 21. These included albums by **Rebecca Ferguson**, **Two Door Cinema Club** and **Nero**. The definition used for this analysis means that artists can be classed as breakthroughs even when they are already familiar names to music buyers. Two examples from last year are **Noel Gallagher's High Flying Birds** and **Beady Eye** – both featuring artists who have already enjoyed widescale success with **Oasis**.

In each year there is a mix of titles, with some that have reached the 100,000 mark in less than a year and others that have taken slightly longer. However, the majority of artists have their breakthrough album on their debut. In 2011 these included **The Vaccines** (see sidebar), **Katy B**, **Ed Sheeran**, **Cher Lloyd** and **Rizzle Kicks**.

Number of Debut Breakthrough Albums

	Debut	Total	Debut %
2007	26	39	67%
2008	35	45	78%
2009	32	46	70%
2010	22	31	71%
2011	24	32	75%

Source: BPI based on Official Charts Company data

Number of Breakthrough Artists

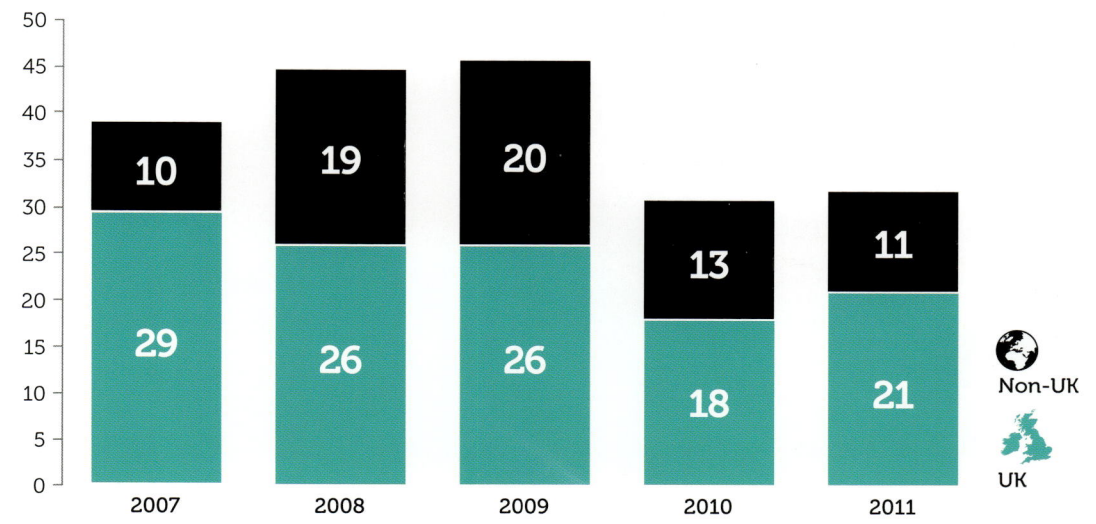

Year	UK	Non-UK	Total
2007	29	10	39
2008	26	19	45
2009	26	20	46
2010	18	13	31
2011	21	11	32

Source: BPI based on Official Charts Company data

Fastest Sellers and Debuts

Now 80 achieves biggest week one sales total

The fastest seller of 2010, **Take That**'s *Progress*, was the quickest-selling album since **Oasis**' *Be Here Now* in 1997, amassing a huge first week total of 518,601. While nothing sold on quite that scale in its week of release – not even **Adele**'s otherwise all-conquering *21* – there was continued demand for the *Now* series which claimed the top three places, the November-released *Now 80* selling just under 296,000 copies in its first week. The biggest week one total for an artist release came in May, when **Lady Gaga**'s much-anticipated second album *Born This Way* reached the shops and sold over 215,000 copies. Two other albums also passed the 200,000 marker in their first week on sale – **Coldplay**'s fifth album *Mylo Xyloto*, released at the end of October, and **Adele**'s *21*. In total 15 albums sold more than 100,000 copies in their week of release, including titles by **Olly Murs**, **Foo Fighters** and **Amy Winehouse**.

Bruno Mars enjoyed the biggest selling debut of the year – his *Doo-Wops & Hooligans* was released in January and did not leave the top 20 for the rest of the year. The rest of the debuts top 10 was comprised of domestic acts, all of whose albums charted in the year-end top 75.

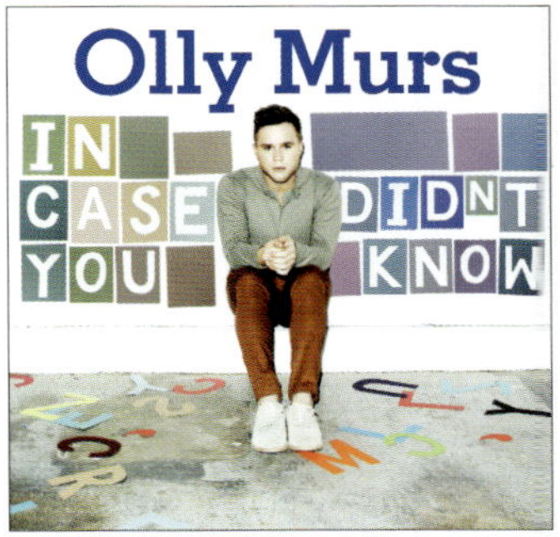

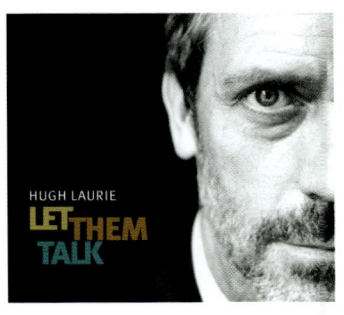

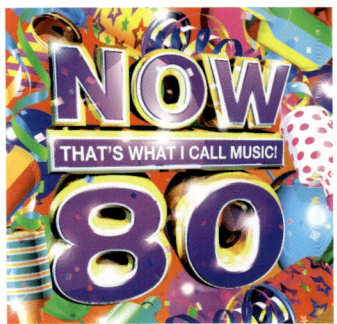

Highest Week One Sales 2011 – Albums

				Week of release
1	Various Artists	*Now 80*	EMI TV/UMTV	47
2	Various Artists	*Now 79*	EMI TV/UMTV	30
3	Various Artists	*Now 78*	EMI TV/UMTV	15
4	Lady Gaga	*Born This Way*	Polydor	21
5	Coldplay	*Mylo Xyloto*	Parlophone	43
6	Adele	*21*	XL Recordings	4
7	Amy Winehouse	*Lioness – Hidden Treasures*	Universal Island	49
8	Rihanna	*Talk That Talk*	Mercury	47
9	Olly Murs	*In Case You Didn't Know*	Epic Label Group	48
10	One Direction	*Up All Night*	RCA Label Group	47

Source: Official Charts Company

Biggest Selling 2011 Debut Albums

				Overall position
1	Bruno Mars	*Doo-Wops & Hooligans*	Atlantic Records UK	3
2	Jessie J	*Who You Are*	Universal Island	10
3	Ed Sheeran	*+*	Atlantic Records UK	11
4	Noel Gallagher's High Flying Birds	*Noel Gallagher's High Flying Birds*	Sour Mash	17
5	One Direction	*Up All Night*	RCA Label Group	19
6	Rebecca Ferguson	*Heaven*	RCA Label Group	29
7	Matt Cardle	*Letters*	Columbia Label Group	54
8	The Vaccines	*What Did You Expect From…*	Columbia Label Group	58
9	Hugh Laurie	*Let Them Talk*	Warner Bros	65
10	Katy B	*On A Mission*	Columbia Label Group	66

Source: Official Charts Company

PROFILE:
Why Pink Floyd? campaign

One of the biggest events in the 2011 catalogue market was the *Why Pink Floyd?* campaign. Aimed at three core audiences – existing fans, lapsed fans and mainstream/gifting buyers – this ambitious project reissued the band's entire catalogue over a number of product tiers.

In late September all 14 of the band's studio albums were released in remastered form as 'Discovery' digipacks (also collected in one box set) and new digital editions. The band's most famous album, *Dark Side Of The Moon*, was concurrently issued as both an 'Experience' edition (with an extra disc of bonus content) and a multi-disc 'Immersion' box set. The next month the new *A Foot In The Door* single CD compilation followed, along with Experience and Immersion editions of *Wish You Were Here*. A three-tier release of *The Wall* completed the schedule in February.

Building awareness took place over several months, with pre-orders going live in March 2011 and promotional activity on the official Facebook page driving the number of 'likes' up from 8m to 17m in the space of a year. Existing fans were engaged with through a combination of PinkFloyd.com, fan sites and social media, with a mobile app also released, while the lapsed audience was targeted via a dedicated YouTube channel and the specialist music press. The mainstream and gifting audience were reached out to through initiatives such as online ads, radio broadcasts, TV slots and streaming events.

"Chart positions were never a priority for the campaign but we were really pleased with them" says **Paul Fletcher, Marketing Director at EMI Music UK**. "Dark Side entered at number 11 and eight titles made the top 200. We've shipped 270,000 units in the UK and 4.5m globally, and digital take-up has been very healthy too. It's been a great success".

Back Catalogue – Albums
Adele drives share growth in both catalogue and new release markets

In the chart and for the purpose of analysis on this page, back catalogue titles are defined as those which were released two years before the year in question – so for 2011 this would mean all of those albums released no more recently than December 2009. Titles from 2010 are classified as 'current' releases.

Originally released in January 2008, **Adele**'s *19* charted at number four in the year-end rundown and sold over 1.2m copies in 2011, two and a half times the tally for its first year's worth of sales. It is very rare for catalogue titles to perform quite so well at this stage of their lifecyle and only one other charted within the annual top 30 (by **Mumford & Sons**).

In total 16 catalogue titles sold over 100,000 copies in 2011, bringing that share of the market up to 32.1% of sales from 29.1% in 2010. New titles – driven by **Adele**'s *21* – claimed over half (51.7%) of all sales, up from 49.0%, with current titles accruing a smaller share.

Top 10 Back Catalogue Albums 2011 and Year of Release

	Artist	Title	Company	Year of Release
1	Adele	19	XL Recordings	2008
2	Mumford & Sons	Sigh No More	Universal Island	2009
3	Lady Gaga	The Fame	Polydor	2009
4	Amy Winehouse	Back To Black	Universal Island	2006
5	Florence & The Machine	Lungs	Universal Island	2009
6	Foo Fighters	Greatest Hits	Columbia Label Group	2009
7	Take That	Never Forget – The Ultimate Collection	RCA Label Group	2005
8	Rihanna	Good Girl Gone Bad	Mercury	2008
9	Kings Of Leon	Only By The Night	Columbia Label Group	2008
10	Paolo Nutini	Sunny Side Up	Atlantic Records UK	2009

Source: Official Charts Company

Back Catalogue Sales – Albums (% down)

	All Albums	Artist Albums	Compilations
Back catalogue (2009 & before)	32.1	34.8	19.5
Current releases (2010)	16.2	15.5	19.2
New releases (2011)	51.7	49.7	61.3
Total	100	100	100

Source: BPI based on Official Charts Company data
Base: Top 10,000 albums

Back Catalogue – Singles
Britain's Got Talent makes *Fast Car* a hit again

Talent shows again had a strong hand in shaping the catalogue tracks top 10 in 2011. Its use as an audition song by several contestants in X-Factor helped **Adele**'s version of *Make You Feel My Love* become a hit in 2010 and it was again the most popular track from her debut album a year later. **Tracy Chapman**'s *Fast Car* was performed by a finalist in Britain's Got Talent and became a hit all over again in April, racing up to number four, its highest ever position. Similarly, **The Goo Goo Dolls**' *Iris* climbed to a new chart peak of number three in September some 13 years after its original release thanks to X-Factor contestant Frankie Cocozza's cover.

The oldest track in the top 10 was *Fairytale Of New York*, originally recorded in 1987. It returned to the top 20 again in December, as it has done in every year since 2005. The most recent to feature was **Black Eyed Peas**' *I Gotta Feeling*, released in 2009 and the first track to pass 1m downloads in the UK.

Based on the top 2,000 sellers in the singles market, catalogue tracks accounted for over a quarter (26.3%) of sales in 2011, up from 24.2%. New releases still accounted for the majority, but share was down to 50.9%, from 59.5%.

Back Catalogue Sales – Singles (% down)

	All Singles
Back catalogue (2009 & before)	26.3
Current releases (2010)	22.9
New releases (2011)	50.9
Total	100

Source: BPI based on Official Charts Company data
Base: Top 2,000 singles

Top 10 Back Catalogue Singles 2011 and Year of Release

	Artist	Title	Company	Year of Release
1	Adele	*Make You Feel My Love*	XL Recordings	2008
2	Tracy Chapman	*Fast Car*	Atlantic Records UK	1988
3	Goo Goo Dolls	*Iris*	Warner Bros	1998
4	Black Eyed Peas	*I Gotta Feeling*	Polydor	2009
5	Snow Patrol	*Chasing Cars*	Polydor	2006
6	The Calling	*Wherever You Will Go*	Columbia Label Group	2004
7	Coldplay	*Fix You*	Parlophone	2005
8	Pogues ft Kirsty MacColl	*Fairytale Of New York*	Warner Bros	1987
9	Elbow	*One Day Like This*	Polydor	2008
10	Nirvana	*Smells Like Teen Spirit*	Polydor	1991

Source: Official Charts Company

Compilation Albums – Sales and Price

Share falls to 17.4% in 2011

Compilation sales dipped below 20m in 2011, equivalent to a 17.4% share of all albums sold. Despite some solid performances – from the **Now** series in particular – only 18 titles sold more than 100,000 copies, down from 28 in 2010. Again there was an absence of breakthrough soundtrack titles – only 1.1m were sold in 2011, less than a third of the 2008 tally – with the biggest seller placing outside the top 300 in the combined chart.

The price of both compilations and artist albums continues to fall, with the average cost to the consumer of a single disc various artists title now just above £5 according to Kantar's survey data. Artist albums now retail for an average of £7.07, down from £7.35 in 2010. Despite the lower cost across the board, however, the percentage of physical album buyers that bought both an artist and compilation title has fallen in the past two years. Although there are several well-established brands with loyal followings in the market, the proportion of consumers that only buy compilations is relatively small – 8.4% in 2011.

Digital took time to gain ground in the compilations market, but its share has now risen to 16.3%. **Now 79** and **Now That's What I Call Xmas** were among the most downloaded albums of the year, with the latter's digital sales amounting to 46% of its total.

Compilation Sales

	2004	2005	2006	2007	2008	2009	2010	2011
Units (m)*	39.0	32.8	30.4	30.5	30.0	25.1	22.4	19.2

Compilations share of all album sales (%)

	2004	2005	2006	2007	2008	2009	2010	2011
Multi Artist Compilations	21.7%	19.4%	18.1%	20.3%	19.4%	17.8%	17.9%	16.3%
Multi Artist Soundtracks	2.2%	1.3%	1.6%	2.0%	3.5%	2.2%	1.5%	1.1%
Total	23.9%	20.7%	19.7%	22.3%	22.9%	20.0%	19.4%	17.4%

Source: BPI based on Official Charts Company data
*total does not include unidentified digital titles

Average Retail Price of Compilations

	2009	2010	2011
Total	£8.87	£8.66	£7.88
Single Disc	£6.21	£6.11	£5.16
Multi Disc	£9.87	£9.66	£8.78

Source: Kantar Worldpanel

Artist/Compilation Album Buyer Overlap
(% buyers, down)

	2009	2010	2011
Artist Albums Only	61.6	62.1	64.9
Compilation Albums Only	9.5	9.5	8.4
Both	28.9	28.4	26.7

Source: Kantar Worldpanel
Base: physical albums

Digital's Share of Compilation Sales (%)

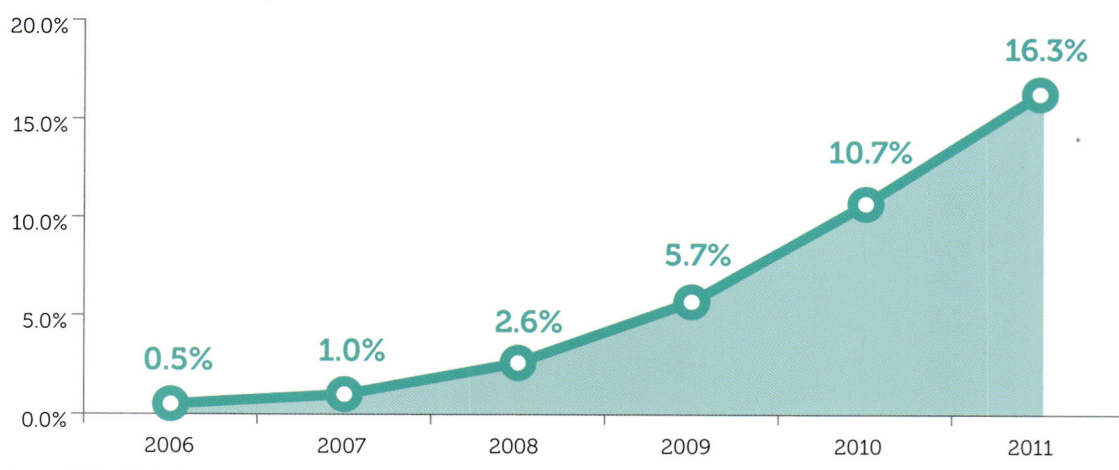

2006	2007	2008	2009	2010	2011
0.5%	1.0%	2.6%	5.7%	10.7%	16.3%

Source: Official Charts Company

Compilation Albums – Sales by Month and Price Category

Budget sector records growth in artist and compilations markets

While the fortunes of the artist albums market fluctuated on a month-by-month basis, compilation sales were down in all but one in 2011. April was the only month in which an increase was recorded, due largely to the later release of the Easter *Now* (*Now 78*) compilation, the only album to outsell Adele's *21* in any of the first six months of the year.

Although there were some strong individual performances, the **full price** sector of the compilations market suffered something of a slump in 2011, with sales falling by over a fifth. As a result its share dropped from 74.3% of all various artist sales to 69.1%, with both **mid price** and **budget** taking greater shares, even though sales in the former did not increase year on year. Budget compilation sales overtook those in the mid price bracket in 2011 and the sector now accounts for a 16.1% share, up from 11.7%.

ARTIST ALBUMS

Sales in both the budget and mid price artist album markets improved in 2011, but the 5.7% decline in the full price sector – which accounts for 64% of sales – meant that an overall decrease was recorded. Artist album sales were up in five months, the highest percentage increase (+6.8%) taking place in June thanks in part to the performance of albums by Adele and Lady Gaga.

Compilation & Artist Album Sales by Price Category (units m)

		2009	2010	2011	% change
Artist Albums	Budget	7.380	6.978	7.134	+2.2%
	Mid Price	21.473	24.441	25.582	+4.7%
	Full Price	71.683	61.775	58.253	-5.7%
	Total	100.536	93.194	90.969	-2.4%
Compilations	Budget	2.426	2.625	3.090	+17.7%
	Mid Price	3.191	3.130	2.831	-9.5%
	Full Price	19.449	16.632	13.269	-20.2%
	Total	25.066	22.386	19.190	-14.3%

Source: Official Charts Company
Note: totals do not match those on p10 due to a small number of unidentified digital albums which cannot be attributed to either artist or compilation albums

Compilation and Artist Album Sales Growth by Month 2011

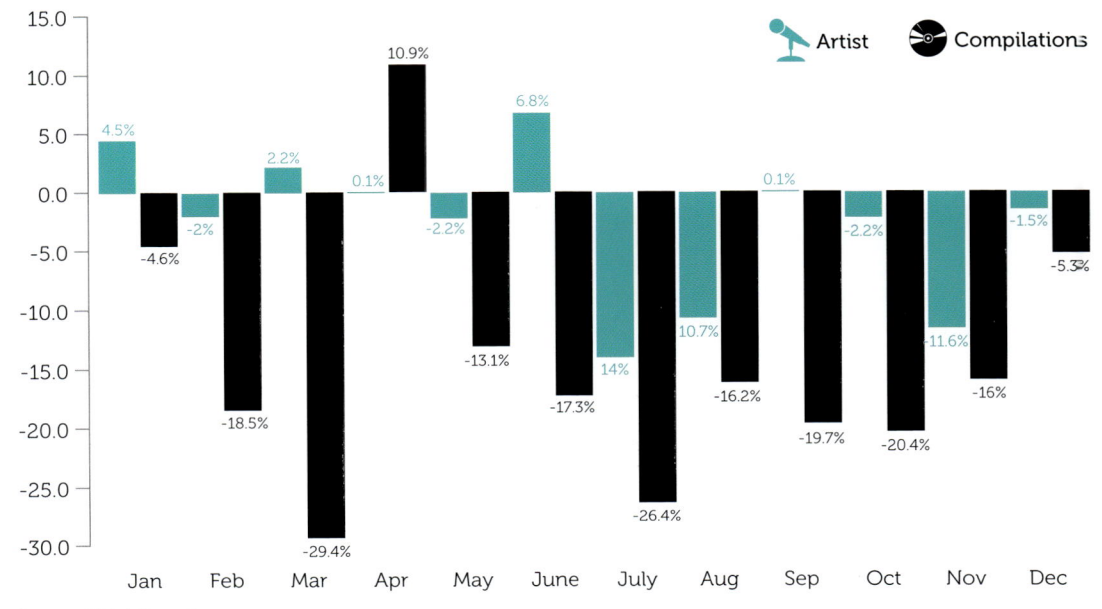

Month	Artist	Compilations
Jan	4.5%	-4.6%
Feb	-2%	-18.5%
Mar	2.2%	-29.4%
Apr	0.1%	10.9%
May	-2.2%	-13.1%
June	6.8%	-17.3%
July	-14%	-26.4%
Aug	-10.7%	-16.2%
Sep	0.1%	-19.7%
Oct	-2.2%	-20.4%
Nov	-11.6%	-16%
Dec	-1.5%	-5.3%

Source: Official Charts Company

PROFILE:
Clubland

Clubland is one of the most popular brands in UK Dance music. Now run as a joint venture between the All Around the World (AATW) and UMTV labels, its first compilation was issued in 2002 and August 2011 saw the release of its 20th volume.

" *Clubland* came from a clubbing scene that was distinctively Northern in its sound" says Universal Music's Naz Idelji.

THIS WAS MUSIC THAT WASN'T BEING SUPPORTED BY ANY NATIONAL MEDIA AVENUES AND AATW SAW A GAP IN THE MARKET TO CREATE A BRAND THAT SOLD TO THE MASSES BEING IGNORED BY MAINSTREAM MEDIA.

Over the past 10 years **Clubland** has evolved stylistically and is now the biggest Dance compilation brand with two sell-out national arena tours, a very successful music channel and summer residencies in Ibiza and Magaluf.

The audience is young clubbers and Dance fans, predominantly aged between 14 and 24 years old. While it was originally catering for an audience that was neglected, the content of the compilations has changed with the acceptance of the style of music **Clubland** specialises in. It's now a round-up of the current biggest and best tracks alongside dance mixes of massive chart toppers. The album's more about hits than it used to be but this is simply following the trend in the audience.

It's primarily sold by TV and that's the main focus for each volume in the series. All television advertising is bought regionally and as the series is particularly popular in the North we're able to reach the audience best that way. We've added in outdoor, online and mobile but TV is still very much the driving force behind this particular brand. "

Compilation Albums – Best Sellers

Now series adds new titles in 2011

Once again the three **Now** compilations released throughout the year were the top sellers, with the November-released volume (**Now 80**) the only compilation to sell over 1m copies, as in 2010. The only title to break **Now**'s dominance in the top five for the year was the ninth volume of **Pop Party**, although the series achieved the remarkable feat of taking six of the top 10 year-end positions. There were a number of new additions to the catalogue in 2011, including the three disc **Now That's What I Call Disney** set and the first editions of **Now That's What I Call Classical** and **Now That's What I Call R&B**.

Some familiar titles charted again, with the new volumes of **Live Lounge**, **Dreamboats and Petticoats** and **Clubland** – which reached its 20th volume (see sidebar) – all making the year-end top 20. Titles making an impact for the first time included **Sugar Sugar**, a three disc set focussing on Pop hits from the end of the sixties, and **Soul City**, a 68-track set including material by **Marvin Gaye**, **The Stylistics** and **The Delfonics**.

Best Selling Compilation Albums 2011

1	Now That's What I Call Music 80	EMI TV/UMTV
2	Now That's What I Call Music 79	EMI TV/UMTV
3	Now That's What I Call Music 78	EMI TV/UMTV
4	Pop Party 9	UMTV
5	Now That's What I Call Xmas	EMI TV/Rhino (Warners)/UMTV
6	Now That's What I Call Disney	EMI TV
7	Now That's What I Call Music 77	EMI TV/UMTV
8	XX – Twenty Years	Ministry Of Sound
9	BBC Radio 1's Live Lounge – Vol 6	RCA/Rhino/UMTV
10	Dreamboats And Petticoats Five	EMI TV/UMTV
11	Clubland 19	UMTV
12	Now That's What I Call Classical	Decca/EMI TV
13	Clubland 20	UMTV
14	Sugar Sugar – The Birth Of Bubblegum Pop	RCA Label Group
15	Soul City	UMTV
16	Merry Xmas	RCA Label Group/UMTV
17	Anthems Alternative 80s	EMI TV/Ministry Of Sound
18	The Ultimate Family Christmas	Go Entertain
19	Now That's What I Call R&B	EMI TV/Rhino/UMTV
20	Ultimate Floorfillers	EMI TV/UMTV

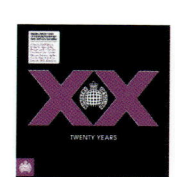

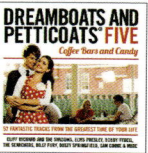

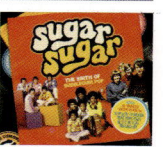

Source: Official Charts Company

Compilation Sales by Type of Retailer and Genre

Pop increases sales share in compilations market

Supermarkets became the dominant retail force in the compilations market in 2009, although it is possible that their share of sales reached its highest point in that year – the sector was then claiming 48.9% but that has decreased in the two years since and now stands at 45.1%. Some of the biggest titles still do very well at Supermarkets, however – six of the top 10 saw over half of their sales take place there.

Specialist retailers have also seen their influence decline although this has taken place over a longer period of time, their last high point being reached in 2006. These stores still took at least a 20% share of sales on each of the top 10 best sellers of the year, however, and accounted for more than 50% on three.

Digital is of course the channel that is growing at the expense of the other retailers, with almost one in every six compilations sold via download stores in 2011. There were impressive digital shares on a number of top sellers – almost a fifth of sales of *Now 77* were digital, and nearly half of *Now That's What I Call Xmas*.

SALES BY GENRE

Nine of the top 10 best selling compilations of the year were classified as Pop, helping the genre's share rise to 46.5%, its highest share this century. Ministry Of Sound's Dance anthology *XX – 20 Years* was the exception although the two 2011-released *Clubland* titles placed just outside the top 10 were also classed as Dance. Classical's rise in share was largely due to the new *Now* title while Reggae's increase was due mainly to the success of budget titles such as *Ska Madness* and *Young Gifted and Black*.

Compilation Sales by Type of Retailer (% down)

	2005	2006	2007	2008	2009	2010	2011
Supermarkets	39.3	37.9	39.4	41.7	48.9	46.5	45.1
Specialist/General	57.7	59.1	57.8	54.4	43.6	41.2	37.1
Independents	3.0	2.6	1.9	1.3	1.8	1.6	1.6
Digital*	-	0.4	1.0	2.6	5.7	10.7	16.3
Total	100	100	100	100	100	100	100

Source: Official Charts Company
*2006 share based on sales from Q2 onwards

Compilation Sales by Type of Music (% unit)

	2005	2006	2007	2008	2009	2010	2011
Pop	33.9	32.3	39.3	42.8	43.4	42.9	46.5
Dance	22.4	27.1	23.5	21.7	22.8	18.9	17.0
R&B	8.4	7.5	7.2	11.1	9.3	13.9	11.8
Rock	12.9	11.4	11.1	9.0	7.3	9.0	7.6
MOR/Easy Listening	8.6	8.1	6.1	6.2	6.8	6.5	6.0
Classical	4.0	4.0	4.1	2.5	2.7	2.5	3.4
Childrens Audio	2.2	2.2	3.2	2.1	1.5	1.8	2.0
Reggae	1.3	0.9	0.9	1.1	1.6	1.1	1.9
Hip Hop	2.6	2.1	0.9	0.7	1.2	0.8	1.0
Country	1.0	1.6	1.1	0.6	0.7	0.6	0.9
Jazz	0.8	0.7	0.6	0.5	0.5	0.4	0.7
World	1.2	1.4	1.2	0.9	0.6	0.7	0.6
Other	0.9	0.8	0.6	0.8	1.6	0.9	0.6
Total	100	100	100	100	100	100	100

Source: BPI based on Official Charts Company data

Music Video – Best Sellers and Sales by Retailer

Music video sales share improves in 2011

Music video sales held up well in 2011, decreasing by only 2.4% to 4.08m. This was especially impressive bearing in mind that the wider market suffered a fall of 7.2%, resulting in music video's share of sales increasing, to 2.0%. There was strong growth in sales on the Blu-ray format with 318,000 units sold, representing an increase of 29.5%, with its share rising from 5.9% to 7.8% of all music videos sold. Of the top 200 music videos of 2011, 91 were available on Blu-ray and

Specialists remain the key retailers in this market, although their share of sales dropped below 75% in 2011. Supermarkets took an increased percentage, claiming majority shares on titles by **Justin Bieber** and **Michael Jackson**.

Take That had the biggest selling music video of 2009 and the band matched the feat two years later with the release of **Progress Live**. Cast recordings were again a strong feature of the chart, with **Les Misérables** featuring in the top three for a second year running, and the 2011-released **Phantom Of The Opera** taking second place. Documentaries on **Justin Bieber** and **George Harrison** made the top 10 as did new live releases by **Adele**, **Andre Rieu** and **AC/DC**.

Music Video Sales by Type of Retailer (% across)

	Specialists & Multiples	Supermarkets	Independents
2007	81.9	14.7	3.3
2008	84.2	12.4	3.4
2009	80.4	16.8	2.8
2010	75.1	21.5	3.4
2011	73.8	22.9	3.3

Source: Official Charts Company

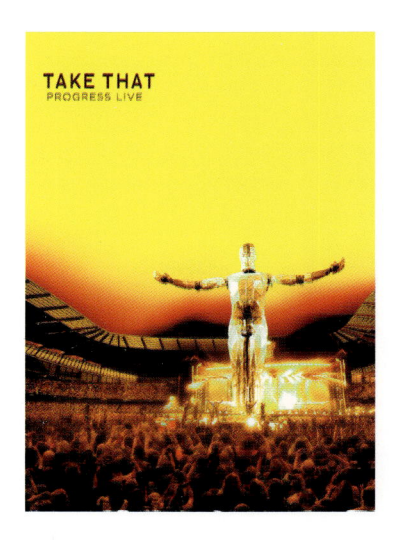

Music Video Sales (m)

	DVD	Blu-ray	Other	Total Music Video	All Video	Music's share
2007	5.36	0.01	0.01	5.37	249.7	2.2%
2008	4.31	0.04	0.01	4.36	257.9	1.7%
2009	4.83	0.15	0.01	4.98	243.5	2.0%
2010	3.93	0.25	-	4.18	223.4	1.9%
2011	3.76	0.32	-	4.08	207.2	2.0%

Source: Official Charts Company

TOP 10 BEST SELLING MUSIC VIDEOS

1 TAKE THAT
Progress Live
Polydor

2 CAST RECORDING
Phantom Of The Opera At The Albert Hall
Universal Pictures

3 ORIGINAL CAST RECORDING
Les Misérables – In Concert – 25th Anniversary
Universal Pictures

4 JUSTIN BIEBER
Justin Bieber – Never Say Never
Paramount Home Entertainment

5 ADELE
Live At The Royal Albert Hall
XL Recordings

6 MICHAEL JACKSON
This Is It
Sony Pictures

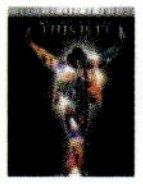

7 GEORGE HARRISON
Living In The Material World
Elevation Sales

8 ANDRE RIEU
The Last Rose – Live In Dublin
Decca

9 ANDRE RIEU
The Christmas I Love
Decca

10 AC/DC
Live At River Plate
Columbia Label Group

Source: Official Charts Company

Music Video – Market Share and Sales by Genre
Music increases share of market in 2011

Film took a slightly smaller share of sales in the wider market in 2011 even though the top four best sellers (the two Harry Potter *Deathly Hallows* titles, *The Inbetweeners Movie* and *The King's Speech*) were all classified in this genre. **Music** was one of only three genres to increase its share, alongside **Children's** (whose big seller was the animated feature film *Despicable Me*) and **Other**, which includes live comedy titles such as those by Peter Kay and Lee Evans, who both featured in the year-end top 20.

The success of Take That's *Progress Live* helped propel **Universal Music**'s share back up above 25% in 2011 although the continued success of Andre Rieu – who had a remarkable 10 titles in the music video top 100 – also contributed significantly. **Universal Pictures**' percentage also rose, to 15.8%, ensuring it moved up to second place in the table from fourth in 2010. Its successes included the cast recordings of *Phantom Of The Opera* and *Les Misérables* and popular titles from Michael Jackson and Cliff Richard.

XL Beggars' first significant share in three years was attributable to Adele's November-released *Live At The Royal Albert Hall* while **Elevation Sales** took a much improved 2.1% thanks to the popularity of their George Harrison documentary *Living In The Material World*.

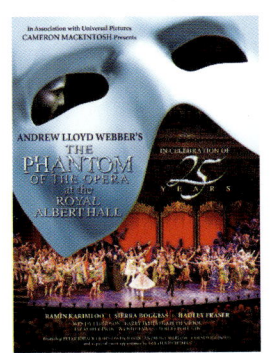

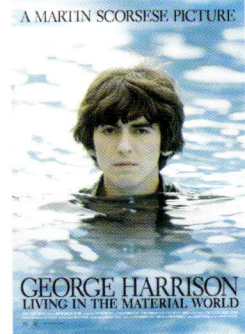

Video Sales by Genre (% across)

	Films	Children's	TV Video	Music Video	Sport/Fitness	Other
2007	68.7	11.7	12.9	2.2	1.4	3.1
2008	69.6	11.1	13.2	1.7	1.7	2.7
2009	67.9	12.0	13.7	2.0	1.4	2.9
2010	65.5	14.4	14.1	1.9	1.5	2.7
2011	64.0	15.6	14.1	2.0	1.3	3.0

Source: Official Charts Company

Music Video Market Share by Company (% units) (% units)

	2006	2007	2008	2009	2010	2011
Universal Music	15.4	16.5	18.4	25.1	16.6	26.4
Universal Pictures	6.0	5.0	5.6	5.7	13.2	15.8
Sony Music	16.1	18.8	22.0	20.1	14.5	11.4
Eagle Rock	5.1	6.5	5.0	4.8	6.1	6.0
Paramount Home Ent.	1.0	0.9	1.3	0.5	0.6	4.1
XL Beggars	-	-	0.1	-	-	3.3
Sony Pictures	0.2	-	-	0.1	14.7	2.8
EMI Music	11.3	9.2	8.0	5.1	4.2	2.4
Elevation Sales	-	0.1	0.3	0.3	0.2	2.1
2entertain	1.5	1.9	1.6	6.2	4.3	2.0
Warner Music Int.	-	-	-	4.1	3.0	1.7
20th Century Fox	0.7	0.9	1.6	0.8	0.5	1.7
Warner Home Video	1.3	1.5	1.0	6.8	2.3	1.2
Lace DVD	0.1	0.1	0.8	-	1.0	1.2
Demon Music Group	3.2	2.0	2.4	1.7	0.3	1.2
Kaleidoscope	-	-	-	-	-	1.0
Opus Arte	0.3	0.3	0.4	0.5	0.7	0.7
Revolver Entertainment	0.1	0.1	0.1	0.1	-	0.7
Entertainment One	-	-	-	-	-	0.7
Chrome Dreams	0.6	0.5	0.5	0.7	0.6	0.6

Source: Official Charts Company

The Year in Independent Music

Adele, Noel, Example and Arctic Monkeys all hit top spot in 2011

It was a one-two on the independent chart for XL Recordings in 2011 thanks to the huge success achieved by **Adele**, whose two albums sold 5m copies between them. Although her 2008-released debut had already made her name, the signs that it was to be her year were in place early on, with **19** rising into the top 10 in the second week of **JANUARY** and her *Make You Feel My Love* single vaulting up to number seven. The following week her new single, *Rolling In The Deep*, charted at number two – a week later **21** was at the top of the album charts, the first of 18 weeks it would spend there in 2011.

■ **FEBRUARY** brought success for Blix Street with their *Eva Cassidy* compilation *Simply Eva* reaching number four, while a stunning BRITs performance resulted in **Adele**'s *Someone Like You* rising from number 47 to the top spot: one week later she occupied the top two places in the album chart.

In the first week of **MARCH** Ministry Of Sound's *Anthems Hip Hop* topped the compilations chart; the month also brought top 10 success for **Daniel O'Donnell**, **The Strokes** and **Radiohead**, with **Duran Duran** and **Joe Bonamassa** also releasing high-charting new albums.

■ **APRIL** gave **Wretch 32** a second top five single of the year, while the first week of **MAY** saw independent releases in the top three of the albums chart, with **Fleet Foxes**' *Helplessness Blues* sandwiched between **Adele**'s *21* and *19*. In week 20 **Friendly Fires**' *Pala* entered at six, while **Caro Emerald** leapt into the top 10, her *Deleted Scenes From The Cutting Room Floor* album going on to sell over 300,000 copies by the year's end. In the last week of the month **The Prodigy**'s live album *World's On Fire* entered the top five, with **Seasick Steve** and **Status Quo** both making the top 10 in the first week of **JUNE**. The month also brought a number one for **Arctic Monkeys**, and a top five album for **Bon Iver** which, in week 25, was one of five independent albums in the top 10. There was also a number one single for **Example** and a top 10 hit for **Alex Gaudino**.

Top 20 Independent Albums 2011

1	Adele	21	XL Recordings
2	Adele	19	XL Recordings
3	Noel Gallagher's High Flying Birds	Noel Gallagher's High Flying Birds	Sour Mash
4	Caro Emerald	Deleted Scenes From The Cutting Room Floor	Dramatico
5	Example	Playing In The Shadows	Ministry Of Sound
6	Arctic Monkeys	Suck It And See	Domino
7	Eva Cassidy	Simply Eva	Blix Street
8	Various Artists	XX – Twenty Years	Ministry Of Sound
9	Fleet Foxes	Helplessness Blues	Bella Union
10	Seasick Steve	You Can't Teach An Old Dog New Tricks	PIAS Recordings
11	Various Artists	Anthems Alternative 80s	EMI TV/Ministry Of Sound
12	Various Artists	The Ultimate Family Christmas	Go Entertain
13	Bon Iver	Bon Iver	4AD
14	Wretch 32	Black And White	Ministry Of Sound
15	Radiohead	The King Of Limbs	XL Recordings
16	Strokes	Angles	Rough Trade
17	Example	Won't Go Quietly	Ministry Of Sound
18	Daniel O'Donnell	The Ultimate Collection	Demon Music
19	Various Artists	The Sound Of Dubstep 2	Ministry Of Sound
20	Various Artists	Anthems Hip-Hop	MOS/RCA Label Group

Source: BPI based on Official Charts Company data

Independent Companies' Market Share (%)

	2004	2005	2006	2007	2008	2009	2010	2011
Albums	19.6	21.3	20.6	22.2	21.3	18.6	17.9	24.1
Singles	21.1	22.7	18.2	20.2	19.3	17.0	15.7	18.9

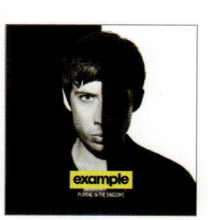

Source: Official Charts Company

■ **JULY** and **AUGUST** brought more singles success for Ministry in the shape of **Vato Gonzalez**, **DJ Fresh** and **Wretch 32**, the latter two hitting the top spot. The critically acclaimed third album by **The Horrors**, *Skying*, was a top five hit for XL and there was also a top 10 album for **Charlie Simpson** despite distribution problems in the wake of the London riots.

■ **SEPTEMBER** belonged to **Example**, who had a number one single and album, while in **OCTOBER Charlene Soraia**'s version of **The Calling**'s *Wherever You Will Go* broke the top 10, peaking at three in week 42. Released on the Sour Mash label, **Noel Gallagher**'s solo debut was a number one and finished the year as the third biggest selling independent release, while in the second week of the month **Daniel O'Donnell** scored his second top 10 album of 2011. There were also hit albums for **Tom Waits** and **The Soldiers**.

In **NOVEMBER** *21* almost dropped out of the Top 10 before, incredibly, rising back up to number one in the first week of the new year.

Independent share rises to 24.1% in albums market

The share of sales attributable to independent labels rose in both the albums and singles markets in 2011. Almost one in four (24.1%) albums bought in 2011 were on an independent label, while the 18.9% share claimed in the singles market was the highest since 2008. Ten of the albums in the year-end combined top 100 (i.e. inclusive of compilations and budget titles) were on independents as were 10 of the top 100 singles, with two tracks by **Adele** featuring in the top 10.

The independents took a strong 22.8% share of artist albums but really excelled in the compilations market, where they accounted for almost a third (30.4%) of sales. They also fared well on digital, with one in every four downloaded albums released by an independent.

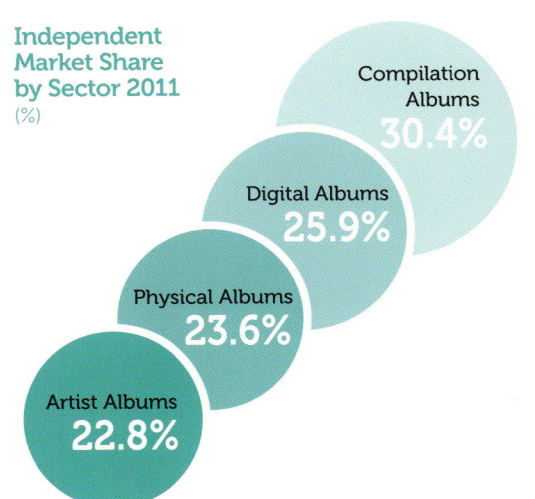

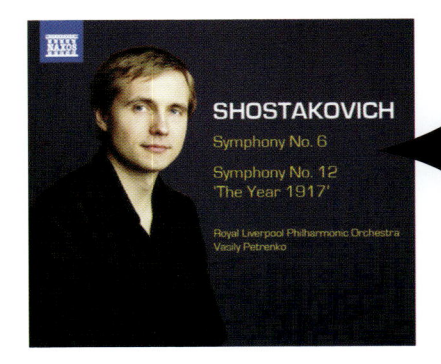

Independent Market Share by Sector 2011
(%)

- Compilation Albums **30.4%**
- Digital Albums **25.9%**
- Physical Albums **23.6%**
- Artist Albums **22.8%**

Source: Official Charts Company

PROFILE:

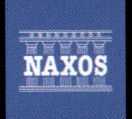

Select is the UK's biggest independent distributor of Classical music, handling the product of over 70 labels including its own well-known Naxos line, whose RLPO/Vasily Petrenko recording of Shostakovich's *10th Symphony* triumphed in the Orchestral category at the 2011 Gramophone Awards.

❝ The two RLPO/Petrenko titles we released last year were both good performers for us", says **Select's Managing Director Anthony Anderson**. "We also did well with a limited re-release of Havergal Brian's *Gothic Symphony* as well as catalogue favourites like Debussy's *Clair de Lune*, *Peter & The Wolf* and Tallis' *Spem In Alium*.

✱ **THE TWO RLPO/PETRENKO TITLES WE RELEASED LAST YEAR WERE BOTH GOOD PERFORMERS FOR US.** ✱

As with a lot of labels there was a decrease in physical sales on Naxos last year but that was offset by download sales including through our own platform Classics Online. Across our distributed labels we saw a strong increase in demand for Classical music DVD and although the general pattern is of a shift to etail and mail order this was less pronounced with Naxos. The independent stores and chains remain a crucial part of the Classical retail landscape, both for new releases and catalogue.

Traditional media – magazines, radio and newspapers – remain important in terms of promoting new releases, but online marketing tools are growing in importance. Naxos' central online presence is its website but this is supplemented by Facebook, Twitter and so on. We've also seen growing sales through our subscription streaming service (www.naxosmusiclibrary.com) and this and our new platform for streamed cultural audiovisual content, Naxos Video Library, have had some strong take-up in the educational sector. We've also launched our first e-books and an iPad application, both initiatives we'll be developing over the coming year. ❞

INDEPENDENT MUSIC

Independent Music – Sales by Genre
Pop overturns Rock as dominant genre

Whereas **Rock** was by far the biggest genre sales-wise in the independent market in 2010 (accounting for over 30%), the 'Adele effect' helped ensure that **Pop** overtook it in 2011. Over one in every three independent albums bought was classed as Pop, with Rock's share decreasing to 26.5% despite the fact that sales of the top five independent **Rock** titles cumulatively amounted to over one million. **Dance** slipped behind **Rock** in share terms despite good performances from a range of titles on Ministry Of Sound, who accounted for the top 10 independent albums in the genre, and MOR's share also fell although there were solid individual performances from titles by Eva Cassidy, Daniel O'Donnell and The Soldiers. **Jazz**'s sales share increased, however, due mainly to the success of Caro Emerald's *Deleted Scenes From The Cutting Room Floor*.

The second graph shows the share within each genre that independent albums accounted for in 2011. The highest occurred in **World**, with artists such as Rodrigo Y Gabriela (signed to Rubyworks) helping independent label share exceed 70%. Companies such as Demon and Union Square had some big sellers in the **Children**'s market and Ministry Of Sound again had a very strong presence in **Dance**. Independent labels took a sales share of more than a third in a further five genres, including the resurgent **Folk** market where Bellowhead, The Civil Wars and King Creosote & Jon Hopkins were among the best selling artists.

Independent Albums – Sales Split by Genre 2011 (%)

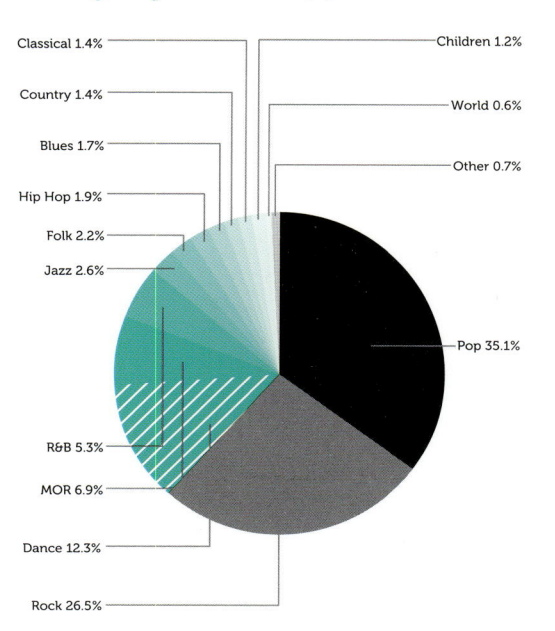

- Classical 1.4%
- Country 1.4%
- Blues 1.7%
- Hip Hop 1.9%
- Folk 2.2%
- Jazz 2.6%
- R&B 5.3%
- MOR 6.9%
- Dance 12.3%
- Rock 26.5%
- Pop 35.1%
- Children 1.2%
- World 0.6%
- Other 0.7%

Source: BPI based on Official Charts Company data

Independent Albums – Sales Share within Genre 2011 (%)

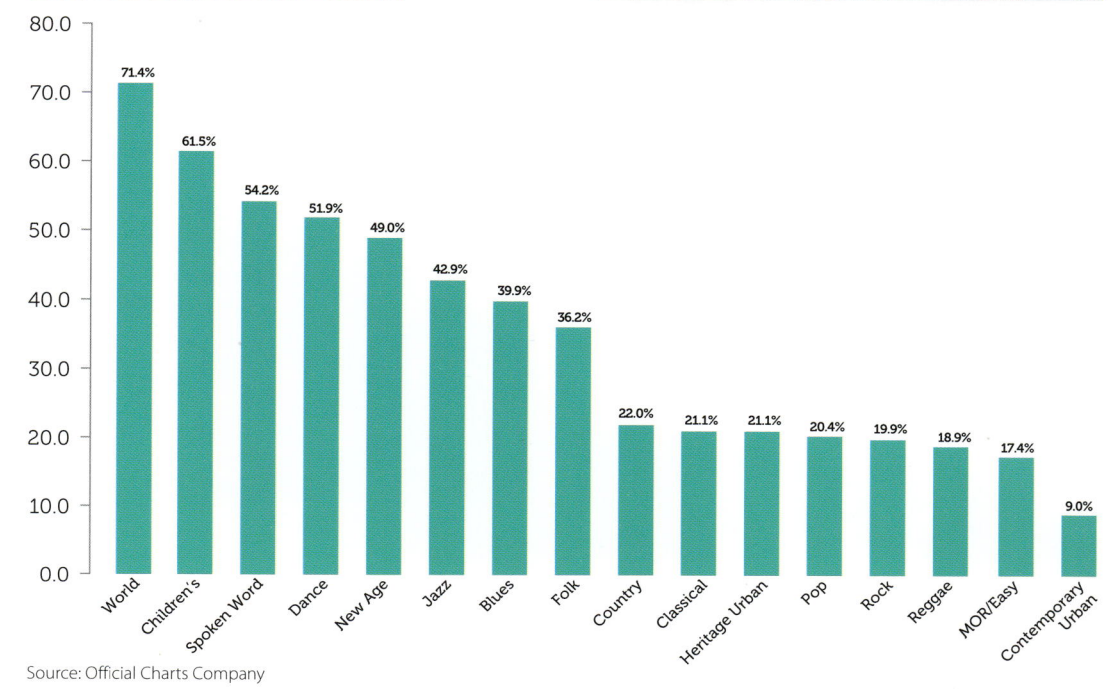

Genre	%
World	71.4%
Children's	61.5%
Spoken Word	54.2%
Dance	51.9%
New Age	49.0%
Jazz	42.9%
Blues	39.9%
Folk	36.2%
Country	22.0%
Classical	21.1%
Heritage Urban	21.1%
Pop	20.4%
Rock	19.9%
Reggae	18.9%
MOR/Easy	17.4%
Contemporary Urban	9.0%

Source: Official Charts Company

Caro Emerald

Market Share – Distributors – Albums

Arvato tops share table again in 2011

Arvato now distributes Universal, Sony and Warner's releases and its share of the physical albums market increased from 56.5% to 58.3% in 2011. It handled five of the top 10 best selling albums of the year, with two (Michael Bublé and Bruno Mars) coming from Warner and three from Universal (Rihanna, Lady Gaga and Jessie J). Other companies distributing product through Arvato in 2011 included Ministry Of Sound, Dirty Hit, Metal Blade and World Circuit.

EMI's share remained on 14.7% with bestsellers including Coldplay's *Mylo Xyloto* and the *Now* series of compilations. The company also provided distribution for the hit albums by Noel Gallagher's High Flying Birds and Beady Eye. The share of sales accounted for by titles distributed by PIAS shot up to 7.9% in 2011 – as previously documented, Adele sold 5m albums in 2011 (4.1m on physical formats) and there were also big sellers for Arctic Monkeys, Seasick Steve, Bon Iver and Radiohead among others.

Other distributors to build on their shares included Sony DADC, who handled product by Union Square and Demon; Proper, who had successes with Bellowhead, The Waterboys and June Tabor, and Plastic Head, whose biggest seller was Nightwish's *Imaginaerum* on the Nuclear Blast label. Those appearing in the table for the first time included ADA Arvato, who distributed product by Dramatico, Blix Street and Because Music (among others) and Essential Gem, who handled Cooking Vinyl's releases alongside albums from Duran Duran and Vintage Trouble.

Distributor Market Share – Physical Format Albums (% units)

	2005	2006	2007	2008	2009	2010	2011
Arvato	15.9	20.1	19.4	46.4	59.0	56.5	58.3
EMI	20.9	18.8	16.5	14.4	14.0	14.7	14.7
PIAS Sony DADC UK	3.4	3.6	3.0	2.7	3.5	3.6	7.9
Cinram	17.1	11.3	9.8	9.1	11.4	12.6	5.4
Sony DADC UK	-	2.9	3.6	5.4	3.8	3.7	4.7
Proper Music	0.6	0.5	0.6	0.7	1.0	1.4	1.6
ADA Cinram	-	-	0.6	1.6	2.2	2.4	1.1
ADA Arvato	-	-	-	-	-	-	0.9
Plastic Head	0.3	0.3	0.3	0.3	0.5	0.7	0.8
Select	0.6	0.6	0.6	0.5	0.5	0.5	0.6
Go Entertain	-	-	-	0.2	0.1	0.3	0.6
Essential Gem	-	-	-	-	-	-	0.4
Absolute Arvato	0.1	0.2	0.6	0.6	0.4	0.3	0.3
Southern	0.3	0.4	0.4	0.4	0.4	0.3	0.3
RSK Gem	-	-	-	-	0.2	0.2	0.3
Imported	0.5	0.5	0.4	0.2	0.3	0.2	0.2
Cargo	0.1	0.1	0.1	0.1	0.1	0.2	0.2
Harmonia Mundi	0.1	0.1	0.1	0.1	0.1	0.1	0.2
Discovery	0.1	0.1	0.1	0.1	0.1	0.1	0.2
Gem	-	-	-	-	-	0.1	0.2
DA Music	-	-	-	0.4	0.2	0.2	0.1
Pinnacle	6.9	5.1	4.3	3.0	0.3	0.1	0.1
Shellshock SRD	0.1	0.1	0.2	0.2	0.2	0.1	0.1
Pickwick	0.2	0.1	0.4	0.2	0.1	0.1	0.1
Cadiz Arvato	0.1	0.1	0.1	0.1	-	0.1	0.1

Source: Official Charts Company

Michael Bublé

Market Share – Company – Albums
Universal tops share table

Universal's share of the albums market dropped slightly in 2011 although seven of their titles featured in the combined top 20 and 56 sold over 100,000 copies, including the new albums by Noah and The Whale, PJ Harvey, The Pierces and Nero.

Sony remained in second place in the table. Its share decreased slightly to 18.6% but 30 of its titles featured in the top 100, including 2011-released albums by Kasabian, Foo Fighters and Will Young. The company also released five of the biggest selling debut albums of the year (see page 41).

EMI and **Warner** swapped places in 2011, the latter's share keeping pace with its strong 2010 performance thanks in no small measure to big hits from Michael Bublé, Bruno Mars and Ed Sheeran. **XL Beggars**' share topped 5% in 2011, a tremendous result. The XL Recordings label had success not only with Adele but also Radiohead, Friendly Fires and The Horrors; Rough Trade (The Strokes) and 4AD (Bon Iver) also released top 10 albums.

Other companies increasing their share included **Domino**, **Go Entertain**, **Bella Union** and **Dramatico**. Noel Gallagher's **Sour Mash** label made the share table for the first time as did **Hospital Records**, who celebrated their 15th anniversary in 2011.

Record Company Market Share – Albums (% units)

	2005	2006	2007	2008	2009	2010	2011
Universal Music	25.5	30.0	32.7	35.7	33.4	33.3	30.7
Sony Music	21.2	20.1	19.0	19.1	22.6	21.0	18.6
Warner Music	12.3	11.4	10.4	10.5	12.4	13.7	13.6
EMI Music	20.1	17.9	15.7	13.4	13.0	14.1	13.0
XL Beggars	1.4	0.8	0.8	1.5	1.3	1.6	5.7
Ministry Of Sound Group	1.4	2.0	2.4	3.2	3.1	2.3	2.1
Demon Music Group	2.5	2.6	3.3	4.1	2.2	1.9	1.6
Union Square Music	0.5	0.7	0.7	0.8	0.9	1.1	1.0
Domino	0.6	0.9	0.6	0.4	0.6	0.3	0.6
Go Entertain	-	-	-	0.2	0.1	0.2	0.5
Sour Mash	-	-	-	-	-	-	0.4
HNH	0.5	0.4	0.4	0.3	0.3	0.3	0.3
Delta	0.2	0.1	0.2	0.3	0.2	0.3	0.3
Bella Union	-	-	-	0.1	0.3	0.2	0.3
Dramatico	0.7	0.3	0.3	0.2	0.1	0.1	0.3
Not Now Music	-	-	-	0.1	0.2	0.3	0.2
Cooking Vinyl	0.1	0.1	0.1	0.1	0.5	0.2	0.2
Cherry Red	-	-	0.1	0.1	0.1	0.2	0.2
Eagle Rock	0.1	0.1	0.2	0.2	0.1	0.1	0.2
PIAS	0.1	0.1	0.1	0.1	0.1	0.1	0.2
Blix Street	-	-	-	0.2	0.1	-	0.2
Weton Wesgram	0.3	0.3	-	0.3	0.2	0.2	0.1
Visible Noise	0.1	0.2	0.1	-	-	0.2	0.1
Snapper Music	0.1	0.2	0.2	0.2	0.1	0.1	0.1
Pickwick	0.1	0.1	0.4	0.1	0.1	0.1	0.1
Warp	0.1	0.1	0.2	0.1	0.1	0.1	0.1
Epitaph	0.1	0.1	0.1	0.1	0.1	0.1	0.1
Ace	0.1	0.1	0.1	0.1	0.1	0.1	0.1
Ninja Tune	0.1	0.1	0.1	0.1	0.1	0.1	0.1
One Little Indian	0.1	0.1	0.1	0.1	0.1	0.1	0.1
Hyperion	-	0.1	0.1	0.1	0.1	0.1	0.1
Full Time Hobby	-	0.1	0.1	0.1	0.1	0.1	0.1
New State	-	-	0.1	0.1	0.1	0.1	0.1
Wrasse	-	-	0.1	0.1	0.1	0.1	0.1
First Night	-	-	-	-	0.1	0.1	0.1
Avid	-	-	-	-	0.1	0.1	0.1
Proper	-	-	0.1	0.1	-	0.1	0.1
Silva Screen	-	-	-	-	-	0.1	0.1
Chandos	-	-	-	-	-	0.1	0.1
Hospital	-	-	-	-	-	-	0.1

Source: Official Charts Company
Base: physical and digital albums
Note: the share attributable to unidentified titles has not been presented in this table

Market Share – Company – Singles

Independents' share grows in 2011

After a dip in 2010 **Universal**'s share of singles sales was back up to near its best, the 34.6% recorded in 2009. Five of the top 10 sellers of the year were by Universal artists (Maroon 5, LMFAO, Jessie J, Rihanna and Jennifer Lopez) as were 40 of the top 100. Over 80 tracks sold over 100,000 copies, ranging from catalogue such as Nirvana's *Smells Like Teen Spirit* to new releases by artists such as Rizzle Kicks and Nero.

Sony's share dipped slightly although tracks by Pitbull, Chris Brown, Aloe Blacc and One Direction all appeared in the year-end top 20. **Warner** and **EMI** retained their placings in the share table but both accrued slightly smaller sales percentages. Tracks by Bruno Mars, Ed Sheeran and Christina Perri all appeared in the 2011 top 20 for the former, while Snoop Dogg's *Sweat* was the biggest seller for EMI.

The presence of two Adele singles in the top 10 best sellers list helped **XL Beggars** record a new share high of 2.8% and **Ministry Of Sound**'s 2.4% was their best result in three years thanks to big sellers from Example, DJ Fresh and Wretch 32. **Domino** and **Demon** both took improved shares in 2011 and there were returns to the table for **Peacefrog** (whose Charlene Soraia single was a number three hit) and **PIAS Recordings**, whose Tiesto vs Diplo single was a top 20 hit in March.

Record Company Market Share – Singles (% units)

	2005	2006	2007	2008	2009	2010	2011
Universal Music	32.6	33.7	32.2	30.0	34.6	33.5	34.3
Sony Music	22.6	21.7	22.6	23.4	23.8	22.7	21.2
Warner Music	9.9	14.0	12.0	14.6	13.1	14.9	13.9
EMI Music	12.2	12.4	13.0	12.7	11.5	13.2	11.7
XL Beggars	0.9	1.1	1.3	1.8	1.6	1.4	2.8
Ministry Of Sound Group	2.2	2.5	2.1	2.4	1.4	1.6	2.4
Domino	0.9	0.9	0.6	0.4	0.4	0.2	0.3
Demon Music Group	-	-	0.1	0.1	0.2	0.2	0.3
Peacefrog	-	0.3	-	-	-	-	0.3
PIAS Recordings	0.1	-	0.1	-	-	-	0.2
Dirtee Stank	-	-	-	0.4	0.8	0.3	0.1
Cooking Vinyl	0.2	-	-	-	0.4	0.2	0.1
Silva Screen	-	-	0.2	0.2	0.2	0.2	0.1
Skint	0.1	0.1	0.3	0.2	0.2	0.1	0.1
New State	-	0.1	-	0.2	0.2	0.1	0.1
Infectious Music	-	-	-	-	0.2	0.1	0.1
Warp	0.2	0.1	0.2	0.1	0.1	0.1	0.1
Visible Noise	0.1	0.3	0.1	0.1	0.1	0.1	0.1
Chrysalis Group	0.3	0.2	0.1	0.1	0.1	0.1	0.1
Curb	0.1	0.2	0.1	0.1	0.1	0.1	0.1
Breakbeat Kaos	0.1	0.1	0.1	0.1	0.1	0.1	0.1
One Little Indian	0.1	-	0.1	0.1	0.1	0.1	0.1
Ninja Tune	0.1	-	0.1	0.1	0.1	0.1	0.1
Fantasy	-	-	0.1	0.1	0.1	0.1	0.1
Hospital	-	-	0.1	0.1	0.1	0.1	0.1
Ram	0.1	-	-	-	0.1	0.1	0.1
First Night	-	-	-	-	0.1	0.1	0.1
Defected	0.5	0.8	0.2	0.1	-	0.1	0.1
VP	-	-	-	-	-	0.1	0.1
Super Cassettes	-	-	-	-	-	0.1	0.1
Dramatico	0.3	0.1	0.2	0.1	-	-	0.1
Blix Street	-	-	0.1	0.1	-	-	0.1
Because Music	-	-	-	0.1	-	-	0.1
Epitaph	-	-	0.1	0.1	0.2	0.2	0.1
Stranger	-	-	-	-	-	-	0.1
Sour Mash	-	-	-	-	-	-	0.1
Sheeran Lock	-	-	-	-	-	-	0.1
Eins	-	-	-	-	-	-	0.1
MTA	-	-	-	-	-	-	0.1
Union Square Music	-	-	-	-	-	-	0.1

Source: Official Charts Company
Base: physical and digital singles
Note: the share attributable to unidentified titles has not been presented in this table

THE YEAR IN DIGITAL

Introduction

Over a decade ago – in October 2001 – Apple unveiled the iPod. It was not the first portable digital music player, but it was the one to push music portability into the mainstream. It was also a trigger event in building the legal digital market that has since moved from downloading to a variety of audio and video streaming and subscription services. While the iPod and other MP3 players continue to sell, the next generation of devices, notably touchscreen smartphones and tablets, have created whole new ways to consume and sell music.

The legal digital market back in 2001, which comprised just a handful of services globally, had yet to get off the ground properly. The past 10 years has seen enormous growth and phenomenal innovation. In the UK, 175.1m tracks were downloaded last year representing 98.4% of single sales and 23.5% of album sales are now digital. In its nascency less than a decade ago, digital now makes up 35.4% of label income and is being spread across a variety of models (there are now more than 70 legal and licensed music services in the UK alone, making it the most diverse digital market anywhere in the world).

Services have come and gone, but the market continues to grow and names like **iTunes**, **Spotify** and **YouTube** are shaping music consumption for the future. Other big brands, notably **Amazon** and **Google**, are expected to launch their next-generation services this year in the UK to create a market characterised by its breadth of choice.

$20.1bn
Predicted revenues from digital music (global) in 2015

Source: Companies & Markets (March 2011)

It has not been an easy journey, but all the key factors – hardware, services, ISPs, telcos and consumers – are now aligning more closely to create a strong and growing market for music digitally.

Developments on social media as well as an increasingly open and experimental API sector are among the areas where foundations are being laid for the next decade of digital innovation and growth. Digital is no longer a niche business – it is a central component of the music industry and continues to lead it into the future.

Open APIs

The most important development in digital music in 2011 was arguably that of 'openness' – especially in regard to APIs (application programming interfaces) and social networking (more of which below).

Back in 2009, the Music Hack Day event was born and a variety of services (including **7digital**, **Spotify**, **Songkick**, **SoundCloud** and **The Echo Nest**) opened their APIs – essentially code enabling pieces of software to communicate with each other – to developers to create new hybrid apps, services and widgets that meshed their platforms together.

Now running up to six events globally each year, Music Hack Day is crystallising a powerful trend in both the developer community and the label world.

Three key events in the final few months of 2011 indicate how the rise of APIs is moving into the mainstream. In September at its f8 conference, **Facebook** placed a huge focus on music-based APIs and how partners could plug into the Facebook platform and reach its 800m+ users globally. By January 2012, over 5bn songs had been shared through this platform.

In November, EMI launched its **OpenEMI** platform to allow developers to build new apps on its data. This followed an earlier initiative when Island Def Jam in the US linked its API to that of The Echo Nest to encourage developers to innovate with apps around its artists and catalogue.

The live industry has also experimented in this area with **Seatwave** in the US moving into ticketing APIs for both discovery and sales.

> ✱ **IN SEPTEMBER AT ITS F8 CONFERENCE, FACEBOOK PLACED A HUGE FOCUS ON MUSIC-BASED APIs AND HOW PARTNERS COULD PLUG INTO THE FACEBOOK PLATFORM AND REACH ITS 800M+ USERS GLOBALLY.** ✱

Also in November, **Spotify** unveiled its new direction with the launch of its Apps Finder within its desktop client player. Launching in beta with a dozen partners – among them The Guardian, Songkick, Rolling Stone, Last.fm, Soundrop, Moodagent and Pitchfork – it made a series of music apps available for users to download, each offering a new type of music discovery or recommendations. The App Finder got a full launch in December and Spotify said it would add new apps for a variety of partners on a rolling basis.

Many commentators regarded these developments as indicative of how the digital sector will evolve. Services may focus on one or two functions and open their APIs to third-party developers and allow them to create a whole new set of tools which users can then bolt on to enhance and enrich their listening experience.

Music Goes Social

Music and social media are nothing new, but 2011 was the year when Facebook, the biggest name in social networking, took the plunge and partnered with a variety of digital music names – including Spotify, Pandora, MOG, Rdio and Rhapsody.

Much was read into the fact that **Facebook** chose to make its move in social music just as **Myspace**, the company that first took music into the social realm back in 2004, saw its user numbers dramatically fall off and parent company News Corp sell it to ad firm Specific Media in June. Myspace is promising a relaunch with a new focus, but through APIs, **Facebook** has been able to solve the social music issue on its own platform by linking with some of the most high profile services of the day.

One new service attracting attention in 2011 was undoubtedly **Turntable.fm** – an avatar-based social music listening and discovery platform where users create rooms where several DJs can set up and play in a tag-team environment. Its popularity spawned a number of similar services – among them **Rolling.fm** and **Outloud.fm**.

Due to licensing issues, **Turntable.fm** is currently only available in the US but its founders are looking to raise more funding and sign new deals to see it roll out internationally.

The social and music spheres continued to merge in the mobile games arena. Previously dominated by non-music titles such as **FarmVille** and **CityVille**, social gaming fully embraced music in 2011. Lady Gaga turned to **Zynga**, the most powerful brand in online gaming, to launch her new album *Born This Way*, with the dedicated GagaVille game. In December, Michael Bublé turned to CityVille to promote his *Christmas* album. In April, Zynga also acquired music game company JamLegend to consolidate its move into music.

Further to her partnership with Zynga, Lady Gaga also announced plans to launch her own **LittleMonsters** social network later in 2012, perhaps signalling a move by major artists to take greater control of the social media experience involving their fans rather than leaning on a third-party site.

Meanwhile **MXP4** moved from developing remix games for specific artists to launching its own range of multi-artist and cross-genre games under the **Bopler** umbrella within the Facebook platform.

Forecasts from Parks Associates suggest that social gaming will generate $5bn in revenues by 2015 (a 500% increase from 2010). The music industry, through the sale of both tracks and virtual goods, will be looking to significantly increase its potential share here in the coming years.

> *LADY GAGA ANNOUNCED PLANS IN 2012 TO LAUNCH HER OWN SOCIAL NETWORK, PERHAPS SIGNALLING A MOVE BY MAJOR ARTISTS TO TAKE GREATER CONTROL OF THE SOCIAL MEDIA EXPERIENCE.*

Lady Gaga

High End Audio

As broadband access, Wi-Fi hotspots and 3G mobile coverage have become more ubiquitous, there has been a concurrent drive to deliver music streaming and downloads at improved audio levels.

Many download services – notably **7digital**, **Beatport** and **Amazon MP3** – have been offering MP3 downloads at 320kbps (described as "near-CD quality") for a number of years. **iTunes** continues to offer downloads at 265kbps. But as part of its **iTunes Match** service (see below), it will offer paying subscribers the chance to upgrade all their audio files to its 265kbps standard.

As part of its upsell strategy, **Spotify** has been offering subscribers streaming rates of 320kbps and other premium services are moving to match this.

The falling cost of streaming-compatible home audio systems from companies such as Sonos, Logitech and Bose are helping to cater for consumer demand for high digital music quality. This coincides with the rise of premium headphones in the market, driven mainly by Beats By Dre whose Beats Audio technology is also being used in a number of devices such as HP laptops and HTC smartphones.

In the download market, there was a concerted effort to court the audiophile audience with high-end lossless formats in 2011.

In March, **7digital** secured the digital exclusive to make the latest Radiohead album, *The King Of Limbs*, available as 24-bit FLAC downloads. This was followed in August by the store opening a dedicated FLAC section on its site, offering 16-bit and 24-bit FLAC files in 32 markets. The company is also offering the FLAC HD format and co-founder and CEO Ben Drury firmly believes that 7digital will be offering FLAC downloads from all the major labels and key independents in 2012.

FLAC and other lossless formats were aimed initially at professional DJs so they could play digital files over sound systems in a way where the audio quality did not break up. Specialist retailers such as **Bleep**, **Boomkat** and **Beatport** (now also offering high quality AIFF files) have been catering to their needs for a number of years, but other stores are moving to offer such files alongside MP3s as a premium tier format. The **Passionato** download service has been pursuing a similar route for its Classical consumers who are increasingly demanding higher audio quality from digital files.

Universal Music also launched the **Groovetown Vinyl** store in April 2011, specialising in vinyl in high audio quality that comes with bundled FLAC files, allowing buyers of premium physical formats to download their purchases as high-end digital files. As it stands, only a limited number of portable devices offer support for formats such as FLAC and WAV but more are expected to come to market in the next year.

Artists and broadcasters are starting to experiment with high-end formats too. In May, **Absolute Radio** recorded Elbow at St. Paul's Cathedral in London and streamed the show on-demand online using FLAC technology as well as HD video.

Streaming Services

Music streaming continued to grow in 2011 and, while Spotify is the UK market leader, increased competition came with the launch of Deezer (the biggest music subscription service in France). There is also scope for further additions to the market, with US names like MOG, Rdio and Rhapsody all hinting at international expansion in 2012.

Meanwhile other UK streaming services – notably **we7** and **mflow** (under its new name of **Bloom.fm**) – stepped back from the on-demand sector and refocused on Pandora-style discovery.

Spotify now has over 10m users in 12 markets and has reportedly paid out over $200m to labels and publishers to date. At the time of writing (February 2012) over 3m of its users are now subscribers paying a fee to access – an increase of 2m since March 2011. To help drive subscriptions, the service placed restrictions on track plays and total listening time for users on the free tier, which has appeared to contribute to a migration of users from the free services to paying subscribers. It was also a landmark year for the service with its US launch finally taking place in July 2011.

✱ 7DIGITAL ARE ONE OF THE LEADING MUSIC SERVICES RESPONDING POSITIVELY TO INCREASED CONSUMER DEMAND FOR HIGH QUALITY AUDIO.✱

New Album Formats

The singles market is now almost entirely made up of downloads but the album market remains skewed towards the CD. In 2011, single tracks made up more than 98% of all singles sales while 23.5% of album sales were digital (up from 17.5% in 2010). The rate of growth is strong, with digital album sales up 27% in what is becoming an increasingly competitive market.

*A NUMBER OF ACTS WORKED WITH THE TABLET PLATFORM IN 2011, INCLUDING SWEDISH HOUSE MAFIA WHO RELEASED A VERSION OF THEIR *UNTIL ONE* ALBUM DESIGNED SPECIFICALLY FOR THE iPAD.*

Digital's Share of Sales (%)

	2005	2006	2007	2008	2009	2010	2011
Albums	–	1.8	4.5	7.7	12.5	17.5	23.5
Singles	55.2	79.3	90.1	95.8	98.0	98.7	99.3

Source: Official Charts Company

In the US some aggressive experimentation has been happening around digital album pricing with Amazon MP3 offering Lady Gaga's *Born This Way* album for $0.99 on its week of release.

Meanwhile, a number of artists used 2011 to experiment with what the album is and how the format can be dramatically adapted for the digital age, new devices and changing consumption patterns.

Undoubtedly the most innovative approach was the one taken by Björk for her *Biophilia* album in July, which was part of a much broader multi-media project that incorporated live performance and the creation of new instruments.

For the album release, she created a 'mother app' for the iPad containing one free song that came with a variety of interactive elements designed specifically for the iPad platform – including a game and an essay about the music. The rest of the album was sold across a further nine individual apps that were downloaded within the 'mother app', each with unique layers and interactive elements. The album got a traditional release too but the creative focus was on how it could work on tablet devices and how this new platform could alter the album experience – both for the creator and the consumer.

A number of other acts worked with the tablet platform too, testing an album's boundaries. Swedish House Mafia released *Until One* an album designed specifically for the iPad and it featured videos, photos and documentary footage. Universal Music also tested the water with iPad albums for catalogue acts including Nirvana, The Rolling Stones and Rush.

Beyond the tablet, The Kaiser Chiefs' *The Future Is Medieval* album examined both what an album is and how it was sold, taking some inspiration from Radiohead's release of *In Rainbows* in 2007. The band made 20 different tracks available and, through a dedicated website, fans could listen to all the tracks and then assemble and download their own 10-track version of the album for £7.50, choosing the running order and the artwork themselves. The added twist was that fans could then make their specific version of the album available on the band's website and they took a £1 share of any sales.

David Gray also tried a new retail strategy by using daily deal site **Groupon** to initially promote his *Lost and Found: Live In Dublin 2011* album as the site's deal of the day in June. It sold for $6, giving Groupon users around 50% discount.

These are all highly innovative attempts to rethink the album in the digital era and they could mark the starting point of a period of innovation around the album this year and beyond.

Swedish House Mafia

Lockers and Next Generation Services

Lockers and cloud matching services have been around for a number of years, but in 2011 three of the biggest names in digital media launched their own music-specific services in the US and they are expected to roll out globally in 2012.

Amazon was the first of the major brands in this market with the launch of its **Cloud Drive** service in March. Users are able to upload their entire digital music collection to the cloud and play back tracks on any connected device – such as PC, smartphone and tablet.

It is linked to its existing download store and users were initially offered 5GB of storage for free, rising to 20GB if they buy music from **Amazon MP3**. Customers can also choose to pay an annual subscription fee (starting at $20 for 20GB of storage space).

Google was hot on Amazon's heels with the **Google Music** service arriving in beta in May. As with Amazon, it was part of a wider strategy and was closely integrated with Android, its smartphone and tablet operating system that is a challenger to Apple's iOS platform (which the iPhone, iPod Touch and iPad all run on).

Users of this service are given cloud storage for up to 20,000 tracks and access on connected devices. It is woven into the Android Market (where tracks can be purchased) as well as the company's **Google+** social network for sharing and discovery.

Finally, Apple made its move into the music cloud with iTunes Match which is part of its wider iCloud platform, allowing users storage space and cross-device synchronisation.

It arrived in the UK in December priced at £21.99 a year. Unlike Amazon and Google's offerings, users do not have to upload their entire digital music collections – or even have to have bought from iTunes itself. Instead, it uses the metadata from all tracks in a user's iTunes collection; they can then stream any tracks (and they are all available at 256kbps even if they were originally ripped or downloaded at a lower bit rate) to connected iOS devices direct from the iTunes store at no extra cost.

In the instance where a track is not available on iTunes, it will be uploaded to the user's storage space and held on Apple's servers so they can download it to any of their registered devices. Also through iCloud, users buying any music from iTunes will see all purchases synchronised automatically on all registered devices.

APPLE MADE ITS MOVE INTO THE MUSIC CLOUD IN 2011 WITH iTUNES MATCH, WHICH ARRIVED IN THE UK IN THE SUMMER.

Bundled Services

There were also some interesting developments in bundled services last year. This is when a music service is included in a subscriber's broadband or mobile contracts. Streaming services Deezer and Spotify both entered into such deals in 2011.

161m
Predicted number of mobile streaming music subscribers (global) in 2016

Source: ABI Research (March 2011)

Spotify had already been active in the UK in this area following a partnership with the 3 mobile network. It also had a deal with mobile operator and ISP Telia in its home country of Sweden in the same year, which was critical in driving its growth there.

At the end of October, Virgin Media announced that it would bundle premium Spotify subscriptions into certain broadband, mobile and TV packages. This was soft launched with select consumers and is expected to broaden out in 2012.

$5.5bn
Predicted global value of mobile music market in 2015

Source: Juniper (February 2011)

Meanwhile in Spain, **Spotify** struck a partnership with car manufacturer Seat to launch an offer which builds a premium streaming subscription into car radios. This follows similar deals in the US between services such as Pandora and satellite radio company Sirius XM and leading car manufacturers such as Ford and Toyota.

Deezer also launched in the UK, having partnered with Orange in France to build its subscriber numbers to 1.2m, making it the country's biggest streaming service. Soon after the UK launch a deal was struck with Orange UK, offering bundled access, a strategy it is expected to build upon this year.

Also of note in the UK was **we7**'s partnership with Karoo, the East Yorkshire broadband portal, to have its music service bundled into a user's broadband package allowing them to listen to unlimited ad-funded streams.

Similar deals are happening in Scandinavia (with the **WiMP** service partnering with Telenor in its home country of Norway) and in both Canada and Brazil (with Rdio partnering with local carriers) among other markets.

However, one of the most high profile bundled offerings was withdrawn from the majority of its markets – including the UK. Launched in late 2008, Nokia's **Comes With Music** took a handset, rather than an operator approach and bundled unlimited music into the cost of compatible Nokia phones. It re-branded itself as **Ovi Music Unlimited** in 2009 but at the start of 2011, Nokia announced it was winding down the service in all but six of the 32 markets it was available in.

Nokia, however, will remain active in music and this will be key to its new range of handsets running the Windows Phone 7 operating system (replacing its own Symbian platform) and its new Nokia Mix Radio (which offers streaming and discovery built into certain smartphone handsets) shows that music will continue to play an important part in its evolution.

Music Video

While YouTube still dominates in terms of total music video consumption (4bn daily streams across all categories globally), a number of interesting and innovative services launched in the UK last year focusing on video content and music.

After its debut in the US at the end of 2009, **Vevo** opened its UK office in April and plans to use London as its base from which to expand into mainland Europe. It is a joint venture from Universal Music, Sony Music Entertainment and Abu Dhabi Media and features content from these companies as well as EMI (but not currently Warner Music Group) and hundreds of independents.

As well as showing promo videos in high definition, Vevo also creates original programming and in 2011 organised, filmed and broadcast shows by acts including Kasabian and Jessie J as well as having programmes such as **The Lift** designed to promote new and emerging acts.

The dominance of **YouTube** arguably makes it the single biggest music platform for music around the world and research by ReadWriteWeb found that eight of its 10 most watched videos are music-based (and the top five – featuring Justin Bieber, Jennifer Lopez, Lady Gaga, Shakira and Eminem – are entirely music). A study by Midem and Nielsen at the start of 2011 across 53 markets also put its scale and reach into context when it found that 17% of those polled paid to download music (yet fewer than 10% had paid to download a full album) while 26% stream music.

YouTube moved further into live broadcasting in 2011, offering streaming from several stages at major US festivals including Coachella, Austin City Limits and Lollapalooza. There were impressive audience numbers for some of its livestreamed gigs, with a Coldplay performance attracting an audience of over 19m.

On top of this, it added its **Merch Store** feature in October to let artist and label partners use their official channels and videos to sell tickets, merchandise and downloads to fans directly. To do this, it struck a number of specialist partner deals with companies including **Topspin**, **Songkick**, **iTunes** and **Amazon**.

While services such as YouTube and Vevo are primarily funded through advertising, steps were made to apply a more direct financial model to live video. In July, **GigSeen** launched in beta in the UK and will charge a monthly subscription fee for access to its concert archive as well as possibly moving into pay-per-view premium access to new events. In a similar vein, Florence & The Machine charged users £3.99 to watch a live stream of their show at the Hackney Empire in London in October for the launch of new album, *Ceremonials*.

Spotify users were able to watch a La Roux gig from London in April and an MGMT show from Paris in October. While audio streaming will remain its core focus, this hints at possible future developments.

Other recent developments in live video included:

* Dublin-based **Muzu** expanding into bespoke live footage in February with its Live & Loud channel, putting two acts against each other in a weekly public vote.
* Mobile operator O2 created the O2AcademyTV YouTube channel, offering live footage and interviews with acts from its branded venues around the UK.
* Vice magazine partnered with Dell and Intel to launch Noisey.com across 11 markets – including the UK, the US, France, Germany, Japan, Australia and Brazil – to offer footage of handpicked breaking acts on a localised basis.

YOUTUBE MOVED FURTHER INTO LIVE BROADCASTING IN 2011. THERE WERE IMPRESSIVE AUDIENCE NUMBERS FOR SOME OF ITS LIVESTREAMED GIGS, WITH A COLDPLAY PERFORMANCE WATCHED BY OVER 19M.

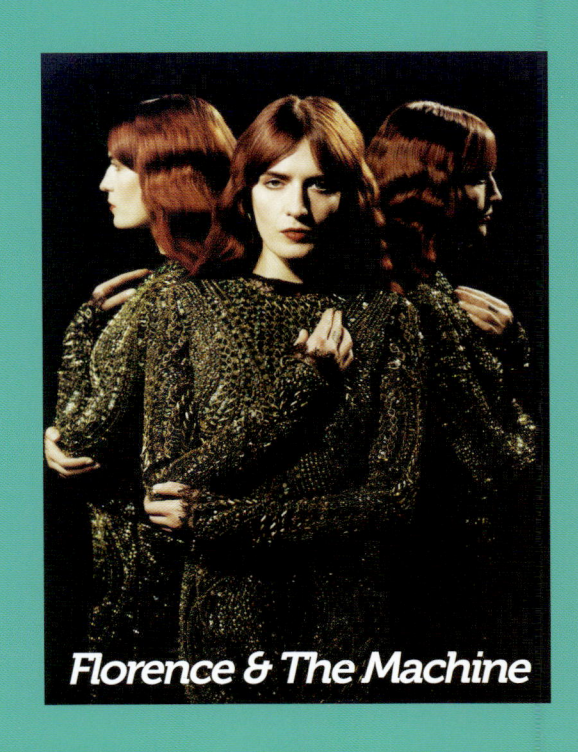

Florence & The Machine

Gaming

Console gaming continued to have a difficult year in 2011, with music title sales falling by 25% to 3.5m units. This situation was exacerbated by the announcement by Activision that it would wind down the Guitar Hero franchise that helped build the music gaming market. While this was announced in February, a subsequent statement by senior executive Dan Winters suggested that the brand was merely "on hiatus" and that new titles would be released.

Music & Games

Units (m)	2009	2010	2011	% change
Music Games	4.179	4.745	3.524	-25.7%
All Games	74.610	62.904	55.442	-11.9%
Music's share	5.6%	7.5%	6.4%	

Value (£m)	2009	2010	2011	% change
Music Games	£95.455	£104.184	£68.676	-34.1%
All Games	£1,681.319	£1,529.634	£1,420.936	-7.1%
Music's share	5.7%	6.8%	4.8%	

Source: GfK Chart Track

Top 10 Music Games 2011

		Platform	Label
1	Just Dance 3	Wii	Ubisoft
2	Just Dance 2	Wii	Ubisoft
3	Michael Jackson: The Experience	Wii	Ubisoft
4	Just Dance	Wii	Ubisoft
5	Dance Central	360	Microsoft
6	Dance Juniors	Wii	Ubisoft
7	Abba: You Can Dance	Wii	Ubisoft
8	Just Dance 3	360	Ubisoft
9	Dance Central 2	360	Microsoft
10	Just Dance 2: Extra Songs	Wii	Ubisoft

Source: GfK Chart Track

One boom area, however, was in dance-based games, built around the motion controllers in the **Wii**, **PlayStation Move** and **Xbox Kinect**. Among the new titles released in 2011 were Dance Central 2, Just Dance 3 and bespoke titles for artists such as Abba and Black Eyed Peas.

The success of dance-based titles is evident in the list of best selling music titles in 2011. Eleven of the top 20 best sellers were dance titles and together they sold 2.2m copies.

There were also a number of popular music-centric fitness titles and the Just Dance franchise had driven more than 25m game sales around the world by the start of 2012.

A US report published by NPD Research found that 80% of dance game purchasers are female, showing a significant new market emerging in a sector traditionally dominated by males.

Mobile and social gaming, however, continued to grow in 2011. As mentioned earlier, Farmville/Cityville creator **Zynga** partnered with Lady Gaga and Michael Bublé to promote their new albums, while users of music games by **MXP4** could play 'lite' versions for free but could also pay to have games adapted around particular titles from the games' licensed catalogues. The company started with a deal in place from EMI (for recorded and publishing rights) and is working on similar deals with the other majors.

In mobile gaming, new title Say What?! was developed by Metropolis Studios and began with a licensing deal with Sony Music. Its iPhone game was built around identifying objects mentioned in song lyrics and indicates how this part of the market can evolve, having been dominated to date by **Tapulous** (which was acquired by Disney in July 2010) and its Tap Tap Revenge franchise.

New and Refocused Services

Given that we are now over a decade on from the iPod, the digital market has grown and matured at astonishing speed. From a licensing and consumption perspective, variety and choice is paramount. There are now over 70 licensed services in the UK and the number is growing, but there were a number of closures in 2011 as well as others refocusing their efforts in a crowded and competitive market. A number of new services arrived, signalling that innovation is still pushing the overall market forward.

One of the oldest names in digital music, initially starting as an unlicensed service that turned the music business on its head in 1999, found itself under new ownership again. After having been bought by Roxio in 2002 and then sold again to Best Buy in 2008, **Napster** was acquired by Rhapsody in the US in October and subsumed within it in November; its rebranding in the UK and Germany (it closed its Japanese arm in May 2010) was delayed until 2012.

rara is another streaming subscription service that launched towards the end of the year initially with just content from the major labels, charging a similar price as **Spotify** and **Rhapsody** (with a web-only tier and a web-plus-mobile tier). It also signed a preloaded distribution deal with HP to be the default music service on its devices. It has artist-curated discovery channels and debuted initially in 15 markets, including the UK, the US, Germany, Ireland, Canada and Mexico.

Two other UK-based services refined and refocused their propositions in the market in 2011. Having emerged in 2008 as a streaming site, **we7** moved away from Spotify-style on-demand listening (although it will still offer premium subscription tiers for this) to instead put its weight behind a streaming radio and recommendation offering. Meanwhile, **mflow** which looked to power discovery by offering users track download credits if their followers on the site bought any of their recommendations, re-emerged in November as **Bloom.fm**, a genre-specific streaming and discovery service.

Away from streaming and downloading, there were many other interesting developments over the course of the year:

* Ticketmaster launched a new Facebook app that integrated with Spotify to recommend upcoming gigs based on a user's listening habits

* Concert discovery site **Songkick** launched its own iPhone app, sending users notifications of upcoming gigs from artists stored in their iTunes libraries and enabling mobile web ticket purchasing

Other notable developments, launches, funding rounds and closures in 2011 included:

* Live Nation acquiring media metrics and analysis company BigChampagne in December

* **Last.fm** owner CBS re-launched the MP3.com site in June with over 1m different tracks (mainly from new and unsigned acts) for free and legal download. It also ties into the Music Manager on Last.fm, which lets any acts upload their music to Last.fm Radio

* Mobile company Research In Motion revealed their dedicated download and social sharing service for users of its BlackBerry handsets across its BBM instant messaging platform. Costing £4.99 a month, it allows users to share up to 50 tracks with others on the service

* In October, digital radio company Pure unveiled its Pure Music service for its web-connected radio sets. It costs £4.99 a month and also works on PC and mobile, with music delivery from 7digital

* In December, **YouTube** acquired RightsFlow (which manages a catalogue of 30m songs) to help it better identify artists and writers whose content appears on its video-sharing site and to direct royalties to them

* boinc (originally launched as Beyond Oblivion) was closed in January before it moved out of beta testing despite having raised an estimated $87m in investment for its next-generation mobile music offering

Retail Spending on Recorded Music

Consumer spending contracts across most entertainment sectors in 2011

Retail spending on recorded music fell once again in 2011 despite the increase in the rate of VAT to 20%. Total estimated consumer spending across all physical and digital formats dropped to £1.112bn, a fall of 3.3% on the previous year. Digital again provided the good news for the recorded music sector, with total expenditure estimated at £378.6m, representing 34% of the overall total. Within digital's annual total:

* Spending on digital albums increased by 24% to £181m
* Spending on single tracks increased by 12% to £151m
* The remainder comprised subscription income, singles bundles, ringtones and music video downloads which together totalled £46.7m. Ad-supported income is excluded from this analysis as it does not represent consumer expenditure.

MUSIC COMPARED TO OTHER SECTORS

There were mixed fortunes for the other sectors of leisure spending presented here. Expenditure on books (in 2010) fell slightly, whilst cinema admissions went up by 5% to break the £1bn barrier for the first time. The strong performance of independent titles such as **The King's Speech** and **The Inbetweeners Movie** contributed to rising box office revenues, although the number one film of the year was **Harry Potter & The Deathly Hallows Part 2**.

Video (excluding music video) on the other hand fell by almost 4% to £1.8bn, despite the increases in Blu-ray sales and digital revenues which IHS Screen Digest measured at £96m in 2011, an increase of 28% on the previous year. Consumer spending on satellite and cable TV rose by 3.5% to stand at £5.6bn and is clearly the largest sector of consumer entertainment spending covered here.

Entertainment software was one of the worst affected with spending falling by 7% to £1.421bn in 2011, as more expenditure switched to digital which is not represented in the data here.

Value of Retail Sales (£m)

	2005	2006	2007	2008	2009	2010	2011	% change
Singles*	£66.6	£40.8	£22.4	£13.1	£9.5	£6.9	£4.0	-42.0%
Albums*	£1,640.0	£1,430.0	£1,184.4	£1,097.6	£926.6	£783.9	£684.9	-12.6%
Digital	£38.0	£70.0	£124.4	£192.4	£267.8	£315.8	£378.6	+19.9%
Music DVD	£102.6	£93.5	£60.5	£49.6	£55.9	£43.9	£44.5	+1.4%
Total	£1,847.2	£1,634.3	£1,391.7	£1,352.7	£1,259.8	£1,150.5	£1,112.0	-3.3%

Source: Official Charts Company/BPI Estimates
*Physical formats only
Note: A change in data reporting methodology has resulted in physical format album spend figures being re-stated from those previously published for the years 2009 and 2010. Music DVD spend figure for 2010 has also been re-stated. Earlier years remain unchanged.

Leisure Spending 2011 (£m)

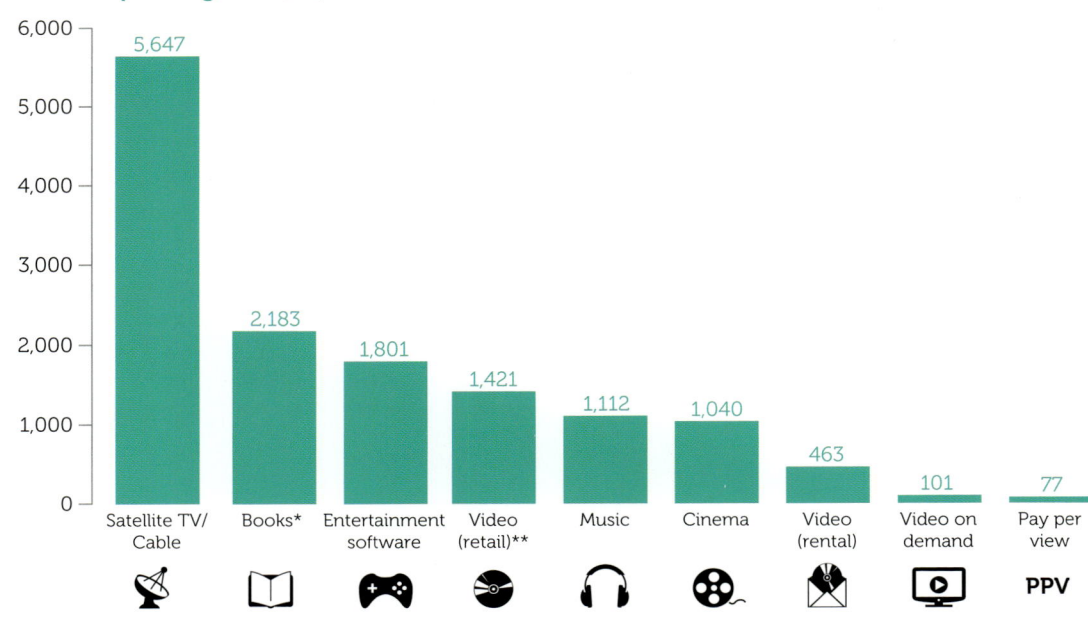

Sector	£m
Satellite TV/Cable	5,647
Books*	2,183
Entertainment software	1,801
Video (retail)**	1,421
Music	1,112
Cinema	1,040
Video (rental)	463
Video on demand	101
Pay per view	77

Source: BPI/Official Charts Company, BVA, IHS Screen Digest, Chart-Track, Rentrak/FDA Yearbook, Publishers Association
*2010 values
**Excludes music video

Retailers Selling Recorded Music

Music retailing undergoes change as home delivery and digital evolve

The landscape of music retailing has altered dramatically in recent years. The table presented here has in the past included the names of many chains which no longer stock music, such as WHSmith and Boots, as well as many who have ceased trading for example MVC, Music Zone, Virgin, Borders and Woolworths. The number of independents has also fallen dramatically from around 900 ten years ago to a third of that total in 2011.

SEASONAL RETAILING

Another feature of music retailing in the UK in recent years has been the increasing number of shops that have chosen to stock music selectively either at peak gifting times of the year or perhaps when a specific album is targeted at their customer base.

The bottom table shows the number of stores within different chains that have stocked music at some point or another during the course of 2011. Some of them, for example The Co-op, have a large number of stores and their combined sales in the run up to Christmas can be significant.

HMV's total of 244 stores does not reflect the number of 'pop-up' outlets it opened in the UK in the run-up to Christmas. Around 20 short-term shops were opened providing a presence in locations that may not have been economically viable on a permanent basis. HMV has been operating these short-term lease arrangements for a couple of years now and they have been successful at attracting the light music buyers who tend to be more active in the run-up towards Christmas.

HOME DELIVERY & DIGITAL RETAILING

Amazon has been established as one of the largest entertainment retailers for a number of years, but companies such as this and Play.com have not featured in analyses such as these where store numbers have traditionally been the key measure.

In digital, however, the market is a little different. The UK boasts a large, expanding number of legitimate services. There are now more than 70 offering the UK digital consumer a range of different types of access and acquisition. These range from a la carte download services such as iTunes, 7digital and Amazon MP3, to streaming services such as Spotify and we7 as well as those that operate within specific genres such as Passionato and Beatport. For a fuller description of developments in the digital marketplace, see pages 56 to 65.

Key Permanent Music Retail Outlets

	2009	2010	2011
HMV	273	269	244
Independent Specialists	293	281	295
Tesco	830	877	892
Sainsbury's	547	557	570
Asda	371	389	514
Morrisons	417	436	470

Source: Millward Brown

Other Music Outlets 2011
(On a Seasonal and 'Event' Basis)

Co-op	3,000
Tesco Express	1,236
Blockbuster	604
M&S	600
Sainsbury's Local	439
Game	380
BP	368
Wilkinson	364
WHSmith	353
Waterstones	300
Matalan	200
BHS	180
Debenhams	124
Disney	57

Source: Millward Brown

Retailer Share – Total Music

HMV still top but Amazon closing in

Tables in this book with the source given as Kantar Worldpanel are based on the purchasing trends of 15,000 demographically representative British individuals. The data presented in these tables are therefore based on consumer research rather than retail sales records.

HMV is still the largest retailer in the recorded music market, accounting for well over a fifth (22.9%) of expenditure in 2011 when its bricks and mortar, home delivery and digital strands are added together. Amazon is catching up, however, according to Kantar's consumer survey data – its home delivery service is comfortably the biggest in the sector and it is second only to iTunes in the download arena, giving it a cumulative 22.4% share of music expenditure.

Digital was the only sector of retailers to see its spend percentage improve in 2011. iTunes remains by some distance the biggest player in the market and accounted for 17.9% of all spend across albums and singles, up from 12.8% in 2010. Downloaded music's share of the market in retail value terms is now approaching a third (31.3%) according to Kantar.

All the supermarkets took a smaller share in 2011, with the sector claiming less than 20% of sales. Tesco still leads the table in this market, with Asda in second place. Home delivery again accounted for over a quarter of all expenditure: Play.com, HMV and Tesco lost share.

Retailer Market Shares – Total Music (%)

	2010	2011	+/-
Music Specialists	26.9	20.9	-6.0
HMV	24.4	19.1	-5.3
Other Music Specialist	2.5	1.8	-0.7
Home Delivery	25.9	25.8	-0.1
Amazon	14.3	15.1	+0.8
Play.com	4.1	3.5	-0.6
HMV	2.7	2.3	-0.4
Tesco	0.8	0.7	-0.1
Asda	0.2	0.2	-
Sainsbury's	-	0.1	+0.1
Other Home Delivery	3.9	3.9	-
Supermarkets	22.7	19.3	-3.4
Asda	7.7	6.3	-1.4
Tesco	9.0	7.9	-1.1
Sainsbury's	3.6	3.0	-0.6
Morrisons	2.3	2.1	-0.2
Digital	21.6	31.3	+9.7
Amazon	4.4	7.3	+2.9
iTunes	12.8	17.9	+5.1
Play.com	0.2	0.3	+0.1
HMV	1.3	1.5	+0.2
Tesco	0.5	0.5	-
Napster	0.4	0.4	-
Other Digital	1.9	3.3	+1.4
Chains/Multiples	2.2	2.1	-0.1
Mail Order	0.3	0.1	-0.2
Other	0.4	0.6	+0.2

Source: Kantar Worldpanel
Base: all music expenditure excepting DVD

Retailer Spend by Gender and Age – Total Music

Supermarkets account for a quarter of women's expenditure

The table on this page looks at the music spend at individual retailers by men, women and the various age groups, comparing them with the breakdown for the total market. Looking at the columns for male and female spend there are two main trends immediately obvious, namely that men spend proportionately more at internet retailers and women more at supermarkets. Over a quarter of women's spend takes place at the latter, compared to just 15.2% of men's music expenditure.

Home delivery and digital retailers together represented 60.6% of male spend, almost 10% more than they represented among women.

Broadly, the overall importance of internet retailers fades as the age of the respective buying groups increases. It should be noted however that Amazon's share increases roughly in tandem with the age of the consumer – it is iTunes' importance to younger consumers (and relative irrelevance to the older ones) that is driving the overall pattern. By contrast, music specialists claim a relatively similar share among all but the very oldest consumers, with HMV representing the lion's share throughout. The Supermarkets are more relied upon by older buyers for their music purchases, with almost a third (30.0%) of music spend by 65 to 79 year olds taking place there in 2011.

Note: Figures in the tables in this section that exceed the total market share have been highlighted.

Retailer Expenditure by Gender and Age 2011
(% down)

	Total	Women	Men	13-19	20-24	25-34	35-44	45-54	55-64	65-79
Internet (Home Delivery & Digital)	57.1	50.7	60.6	66.4	68.9	62.9	55.6	52.3	43.7	45.9
Amazon	22.4	20.7	23.4	16.3	18.3	21.5	24.8	25.8	23.0	26.8
iTunes	17.9	16.9	18.4	33.0	31.9	24.0	13.7	8.9	7.5	4.7
HMV	3.8	3.3	4.1	5.3	5.5	5.0	3.5	3.2	1.7	2.1
Play.com	3.7	3.6	3.8	2.5	4.2	4.1	4.8	3.9	3.1	2.5
Tesco	1.3	0.9	1.5	1.3	1.1	1.4	1.2	1.9	0.6	0.8
Asda	0.2	0.3	0.2	-	0.1	0.2	0.3	0.3	0.1	0.2
Sainsbury's	0.2	0.1	0.2	0.1	0.1	0.1	0.1	0.3	-	0.1
Other Online	7.6	4.9	9.0	7.9	7.7	6.6	7.2	8.0	7.7	8.7
Music Specialists	20.9	20.2	21.3	24.4	19.9	18.8	20.3	20.8	24.9	14.7
HMV	19.1	19.0	19.1	23.6	18.6	16.9	18.2	18.8	22.1	13.5
Other Music Specialist	1.8	1.1	2.2	0.8	1.3	1.9	2.1	2.0	2.8	1.2
Supermarkets	19.3	26.6	15.2	7.9	9.9	16.5	22.2	23.9	26.6	30.0
Tesco	7.9	11.2	6.0	4.1	3.6	6.1	9.3	8.8	11.3	13.8
Asda	6.3	9.0	4.7	2.5	3.2	6.6	7.5	7.8	7.6	7.6
Sainsbury's	3.0	4.0	2.5	0.9	1.5	2.1	3.5	4.3	4.8	4.4
Morrisons	2.1	2.4	1.9	0.5	1.5	1.7	1.8	3.0	2.9	4.1
Chains/Multiples	2.1	2.1	2.1	0.8	0.6	1.4	1.4	2.6	3.7	7.4
Mail Order	0.1	0.1	0.1	-	-	-	-	-	0.2	0.6
Other	0.6	0.3	0.7	0.5	0.7	0.4	0.4	0.4	0.8	1.5

Source: Kantar Worldpanel
Base: all music expenditure excepting Music Video

Retailer Spend by Lifestage Group – Total Music

Internet retail most popular with students, young singles and couples

While Amazon takes the largest share of spend in the home delivery and digital retail sector, iTunes attracts a greater proportion of spend among children (respondents aged under 18) and students, and is a close second with younger singles and couples.

HMV accounts for over a quarter of the music expenditure by children and over a fifth of that by students and older singles. The share that supermarkets claim varies greatly, from only 6.9% among students to 28.3% of music spend by families, with Tesco attracting over 10% by families and couples aged 45 and over.

The internet retailers have seen their share increase rapidly, and across all age groups. In 2009 they accounted for over half of music spend in only two of the seven lifestage groups (students and younger couples); by 2011 that had risen to six. Across that period both the specialists and supermarkets have seen their share decrease in every group; in 2009 the former accounted for over a quarter of spend in five groups but that decreased to just one (children) in 2011.

Retailer Expenditure by Lifestage Group 2011
(% down)

	Total	Children (<18)	Students	Families	Younger Singles (<45)	Older Singles (45+)	Younger Couples (<45)	Older Couples (45+)
Internet (Home Delivery & Digital)	**57.1**	**61.1**	**69.7**	**52.2**	**64.9**	**52.3**	**62.0**	**47.5**
Amazon	22.4	13.2	20.1	20.6	24.3	26.9	23.6	25.1
iTunes	17.9	36.0	28.4	15.0	22.1	7.3	22.7	7.6
HMV	3.8	2.9	6.6	3.7	4.7	3.4	4.4	2.0
Play.com	3.7	1.4	4.5	5.3	3.3	3.4	4.0	3.0
Tesco	1.3	1.0	1.2	1.5	1.3	1.3	1.0	1.2
Asda	0.2	-	-	0.5	0.2	0.2	0.1	0.1
Sainsbury's	0.2	-	0.3	0.2	0.1	0.1	0.2	0.2
Other Online	7.6	6.6	8.6	5.4	8.9	9.7	6.0	8.3
Music Specialists	**20.9**	**27.8**	**22.0**	**17.9**	**20.0**	**24.0**	**21.9**	**19.6**
HMV	19.1	26.6	20.7	17.0	18.0	20.0	18.9	18.1
Other Music Specialist	1.8	1.2	1.3	0.9	2.0	4.0	3.0	1.5
Supermarkets	**19.3**	**9.7**	**6.9**	**28.3**	**13.1**	**19.0**	**14.3**	**27.3**
Tesco	7.9	4.2	3.1	11.8	5.1	9.8	5.1	10.3
Asda	6.3	3.7	2.3	9.2	4.9	5.1	5.4	8.3
Sainsbury's	3.0	1.0	0.7	4.3	2.3	2.8	1.8	5.0
Morrisons	2.1	0.8	0.7	2.9	0.9	1.2	2.0	3.7
Chains/Multiples	**2.1**	**0.9**	**0.8**	**1.0**	**1.6**	**3.4**	**1.6**	**4.7**
Mail Order	**0.1**	-	-	-	-	**0.2**	-	**0.2**
Other	**0.6**	**0.5**	**0.6**	**0.5**	**0.4**	**1.0**	**0.2**	**0.7**

Source: Kantar Worldpanel
Base: all music expenditure excepting Music Video

Retailer Consumer Profile – Total Music
Tesco and Asda attract highest share of spend by women

This table looks at the customer profile of each retail group and the individual retailers shares within them. It shows, for example, that while Tesco stores are one of the few to attract a greater share of spend by women, men account for over three quarters of expenditure generated by their online offer, the highest percentage of any internet retailer in Kantar's sample. Men are responsible for at least 66% of spend at all the home delivery and digital retailers but women's expenditure is greater at both Tesco and Asda stores – overall though, women's share in the supermarket sector is decreasing, from 53.8% in 2009 to 49.3% in 2011.

Buyers aged between 25 and 44 make up the two biggest spending groups in the internet category, although teens now claim 17.7% of the total, up from 14.6% a year previously. These youngest customers account for over a quarter of all money spent on music at iTunes and a fifth of that taking place at HMV's digital and home delivery portals. Play.com appears to appeal to a slightly older demographic, with over a quarter of spend attributable to buyers aged between 35 and 44. This age group also claim the biggest share at Tesco and Asda although the next oldest group (45 to 54) are the most important to Sainsbury's and Morrisons according to Kantar's data.

Retailer Consumer Profile 2011

(% across)	Female	Male	13-19	20-24	25-34	35-44	45-54	55-64	65-79
Total Market	35.7	64.3	15.2	9.2	17.7	20.5	18.7	11.7	7.0
Internet (Home Delivery & Digital)	31.8	68.2	17.7	11.1	19.5	20.0	17.1	9.0	5.6
Amazon	33.0	67.0	11.0	7.5	17.0	22.6	21.5	12.1	8.3
iTunes	33.7	66.3	28.0	16.4	23.8	15.7	9.3	5.0	1.8
HMV	30.8	69.2	20.8	13.1	22.9	18.5	15.5	5.2	3.9
Play.com	34.0	66.0	10.0	10.4	19.5	26.5	19.2	9.8	4.6
Tesco	26.2	73.8	15.1	7.8	19.7	20.1	27.3	5.6	4.3
Other Online	23.9	76.1	13.4	8.9	14.4	20.8	20.9	13.3	8.3
Music Specialists	34.5	65.5	17.7	8.8	16.0	19.9	18.6	14.0	4.9
HMV	35.7	64.3	18.8	9.0	15.7	19.5	18.4	13.6	4.9
Other Music Specialist	22.5	77.5	7.0	6.6	18.6	24.0	20.9	18.4	4.5
Supermarkets	49.3	50.7	6.3	4.7	15.2	23.6	23.1	16.2	10.8
Tesco	50.6	49.4	7.9	4.3	13.8	24.2	20.8	16.9	12.2
Asda	51.4	48.6	6.0	4.7	18.7	24.6	23.3	14.2	8.5
Sainsbury's	46.9	53.1	4.5	4.5	12.3	23.9	26.2	18.4	10.2
Morrisons	41.4	58.6	3.8	6.7	14.3	18.1	27.0	16.5	13.7
Chains/Multiples	35.9	64.1	6.0	2.4	11.3	13.6	22.6	20.1	24.0

Source: Kantar Worldpanel
Base: all music expenditure excepting Music Video

Retailer Share – Artist and Compilation Albums

HMV claims greatest share in both artist and compilation CD markets

Around four in every 10 physical artist albums was purchased through a home delivery channel in 2011. Amazon was the most popular destination by far among these retailers, claiming 22.9% of all expenditure on artist CDs, although HMV accounted for the single biggest share of sales in the artist albums market (28.7%). The albums by **Coldplay** and **Ed Sheeran** both saw over half of their CD sales come through specialist retailers, while more than 60% of the physical sales of the albums by **Florence & The Machine** and **Amy Winehouse** took place there.

Supermarkets collectively took a 41.8% share of physical compilation albums expenditure compared to their 25.3% in the artist albums market. Tesco was second only to HMV in 2011, claiming an 18.0% share of spend, and over 70% of the CD sales of **Now 78** and **Now 79** took place at supermarkets, who also claimed majority physical shares on some best selling artist albums, such as **Adele**'s *21* and **Rihanna**'s *Loud*. Online retailers fared slightly less well on compilations, with only the home delivery arms of the supermarkets taking a greater share of expenditure than they accounted for in the artist albums market.

Retailer Share – Artist and Compilation Albums 2011 (% down)

Artist Albums	
Home Delivery	**39.2**
Amazon	22.9
Play.com	5.3
HMV	3.6
Tesco	0.9
Asda	0.2
Sainsbury's	0.2
Other Home Delivery	6.1
Music Specialists	**31.5**
HMV	28.7
Other Music Specialist	2.8
Supermarkets	**25.3**
Tesco	10.2
Asda	8.5
Sainsbury's	4.0
Morrisons	2.7
Chains/Multiples	**3.1**
Other	**0.8**

Compilation Albums	
Home Delivery	**30.0**
Amazon	16.9
Play.com	4.0
HMV	2.2
Tesco	2.1
Asda	0.6
Sainsbury's	0.2
Other Home Delivery	4.0
Music Specialists	**24.3**
HMV	22.6
Other Music Specialist	1.6
Supermarkets	**41.8**
Tesco	18.0
Asda	12.3
Sainsbury's	6.7
Morrisons	4.8
Chains/Multiples	**3.0**
Other	**0.9**

Source: Kantar Worldpanel
Base: physical albums expenditure

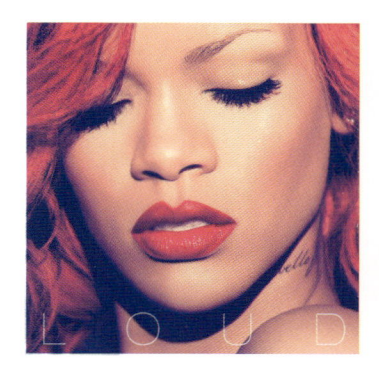

Source: Kantar Worldpanel
Base: physical albums expenditure

Retailers' Genre Profile

Pop still dominant at supermarkets

The table on this page looks at each retailer in terms of the albums purchased there and in which genre they are classified. As no full-year data is available on digital purchase by genre, download-only retailers such as iTunes are omitted.

As might be expected, the mix of music expenditure at supermarkets is very heavily weighted towards pop – even at Tesco's home delivery arm. Close to half of music spend at these shops is on Pop albums, with Rock only just edging out MOR at most of them. At the specialists over a third of customer spend is on Rock CDs and Pop takes second place both there and at every home delivery retailer except Tesco.

R&B and MOR both take their strongest shares at the supermarkets. The former achieved a 10% share of spend at Asda, with MOR accounting for over 10% at each supermarket except Asda. Dance was responsible for over 5% of CD spend at HMV.co.uk, but took a slightly smaller 4% at its stores. Classical took a strong 5.6% share at home delivery retailers, with 6% of spend at Amazon attributable to albums in the genre.

Retailers' Genre Profile 2011 (% across)

	Pop	Rock	R&B	MOR / Easy	Dance	Hip Hop	Classical	Folk	Country	Jazz	Blues	Soul	Other
Internet (Home Delivery)	27.0	32.1	4.5	7.8	4.0	1.8	5.6	2.5	2.1	2.3	1.4	1.4	7.5
Amazon	26.1	31.3	4.4	9.0	4.1	1.8	6.0	2.9	2.6	3.0	1.6	1.7	5.6
Play.com	32.1	39.0	5.9	6.0	3.3	1.4	2.8	1.1	1.6	0.7	0.9	1.3	3.8
HMV	29.9	35.8	6.1	4.8	5.2	3.4	4.7	1.0	1.0	1.4	0.9	1.0	4.8
Tesco	51.0	23.4	5.5	5.9	1.6	0.8	4.6	0.5	0.1	0.6	0.8	0.5	4.7
Music Specialists	27.4	37.0	5.9	5.9	4.2	2.8	4.4	1.3	1.5	1.4	1.6	1.1	5.5
HMV	28.8	35.8	6.3	6.2	4.0	2.9	4.4	1.1	1.4	1.2	1.6	1.0	5.2
Other Music Specialists	13.1	50.0	2.0	3.2	6.5	1.5	3.4	3.5	1.5	3.5	1.7	1.7	8.4
Supermarkets	48.4	15.6	8.4	12.4	3.4	0.8	2.5	0.6	1.1	0.9	1.1	0.8	4.1
Tesco	49.4	14.3	7.7	14.1	2.9	0.7	2.1	0.6	0.9	0.9	1.5	0.4	4.5
Asda	47.4	17.4	10.0	9.8	4.3	1.2	1.7	0.8	1.2	0.5	0.8	1.0	4.0
Sainsbury's	47.7	16.0	6.6	12.4	1.9	0.6	5.8	0.4	1.6	1.5	1.0	0.7	3.9
Morrisons	49.3	14.6	9.0	13.8	4.5	0.3	1.8	0.5	0.6	0.7	0.6	1.5	2.9

Source: Kantar Worldpanel
Base: physical music expenditure

Retailer Loyalty

Internet shoppers are most loyal group in 2011

One of the measures provided in Kantar's survey data that is new to the yearbook is retailer loyalty. In the data on this page it is measured as the percentage of each sector or retailer's shoppers that only purchase music from them. The bar chart shows that in 2011 61.2% of buyers who used internet retailers remained completely loyal to that sector in terms of their total music spend. There is a degree of 'shopping around' within this retail group, however – the highest percentage of loyal buyers accounted for by any individual retailer in this sector is 31.9%, so clearly customers are using more than one to make all their purchases.

Loyalty (by this measurement) is slightly lower in the specialist sector – just over a quarter (26.3%) of those who shop there use these stores exclusively for music – but HMV accounts for most of the needs of this channel's customer base. Supermarkets claim all of the spend of just under a third (32.2%) of their music-buying customers but, as the table shows, this loyalty has fluctuated over the past two years. By contrast, more and more internet buyers are becoming completely loyal to that channel.

Retailer Loyalty (% buyers)

	2009	2010	2011
Internet (Home Delivery & Digital)	56.1	58.0	61.2
Amazon	30.1	27.6	31.9
iTunes	28.5	26.4	30.7
Play.com	19.5	17.6	17.7
HMV	13.1	9.3	11.0
Other Online	18.6	15.4	13.8
Music Specialists	27.5	26.9	26.3
HMV	26.8	25.6	25.8
Other Music Specialists	11.9	15.7	13.8
Supermarkets	36.2	31.9	32.2
Tesco	28.8	22.4	23.9
Asda	25.9	26.3	28.0
Sainsbury's	24.6	20.9	20.9
Morrisons	24.2	23.0	22.6
Chains/Multiples	24.7	18.7	22.1

Source: Kantar Worldpanel
Base: total music

Retailer Loyalty 2011 (% buyers)

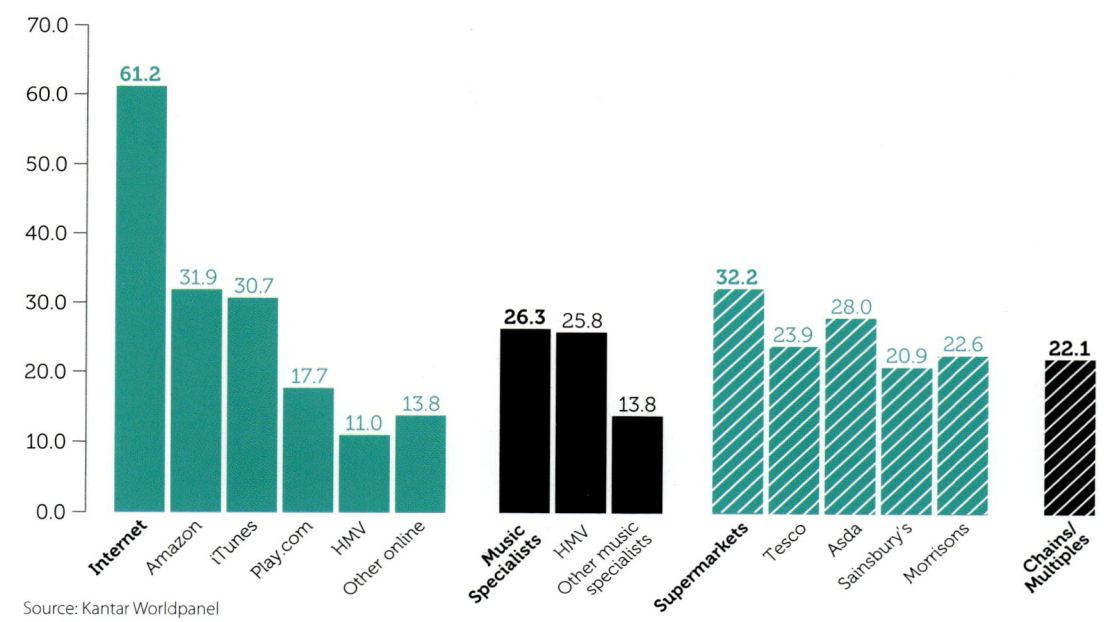

Retailer	%
Internet	61.2
Amazon	31.9
iTunes	30.7
Play.com	17.7
HMV	11.0
Other online	13.8
Music Specialists	26.3
HMV	25.8
Other music specialists	13.8
Supermarkets	32.2
Tesco	23.9
Asda	28.0
Sainsbury's	20.9
Morrisons	22.6
Chains/Multiples	22.1

Source: Kantar Worldpanel

Impulse Purchasing

Planned purchases account for majority but impulse buy percentage is rising

Another data set new to this edition of the yearbook is that which looks at impulse purchasing. All Kantar's survey respondents are asked to record whether each music purchase was made on a planned or an impulse basis, which gives a good idea not just of patterns across the market as a whole but within individual retailers and retail sectors.

The overall percentage of planned album purchases is greater than those made on impulse, although this has been decreasing in recent years, falling from 58% in 2009 to 55.7% in 2011. Impulse purchasing is actually accounting for an increasing share of music bought in every sector, rising from 48.2% at supermarkets in 2009 to 54.9% in 2011.

Planned purchases are far more common in the home delivery and digital sectors, where they account for over two thirds by volume (68.3%), rising to almost three quarters at retailers such as Amazon and Play.com. Impulse decisions make for the majority of purchases at both music specialists and supermarkets, however – the share tops 60% at Sainsbury's.

Men are slightly more impulsive – they account for 66% of spend on unplanned music purchases, compared with the 64.3% they represent in the overall music market. There is a slight younger bias demographically, with spend by buyers under 35 comprising 43.7% in terms of impulse purchases, against 42.1% in the overall market. C1 and DE buyers also account for a slightly greater share of impulse spend than they do for planned purchases.

Impulse/Planned Purchasing Split 2011
(% volume, across)

	Impulse	Planned
Total Market	44.3	55.7
Internet (Home Delivery & Digital)	31.7	68.3
Amazon	28.0	72.0
iTunes	34.1	65.9
Play.com	25.8	74.2
HMV	33.4	66.6
Tesco	32.8	67.2
Other Online	40.7	59.3
Music Specialists	56.2	43.8
HMV	52.8	47.2
Other Music Specialists	78.3	21.7
Supermarkets	54.9	45.1
Tesco	54.4	45.6
Asda	51.5	48.5
Sainsbury's	61.9	38.1
Morrisons	55.0	45.0
Chains/Multiples	79.8	20.2

Source: Kantar Worldpanel
Base: all albums

Percentage of Albums Bought on Impulse
(% volume)

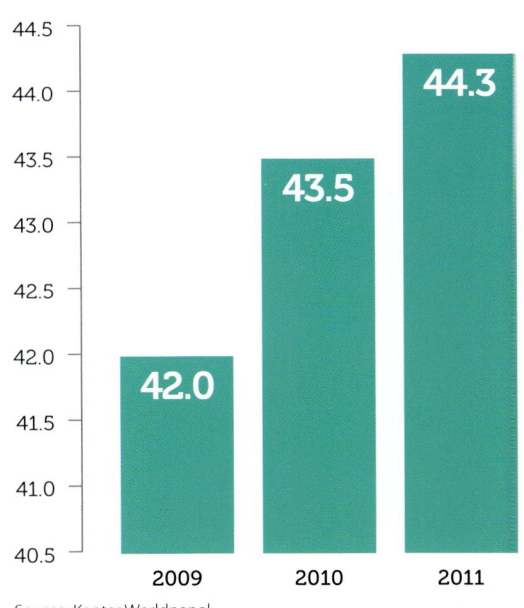

Year	%
2009	42.0
2010	43.5
2011	44.3

Source: Kantar Worldpanel

Impulse Purchasers – Demographics 2011 (% spend across)

	Women	Men	13-19	20-24	25-34	35-44	45-54	55-64	65-79	AB	C1	C2	DE
Total Market	35.7	64.3	15.2	9.2	17.7	20.5	18.7	11.7	7.0	20.3	38.1	22.3	19.2
Impulse	34.0	66.0	15.1	10.2	18.4	19.1	18.3	11.9	7.0	19.8	38.7	21.9	19.6
Planned	36.8	63.2	15.2	8.6	17.3	21.4	18.9	11.6	7.0	20.5	37.8	22.6	19.0

Source: Kantar Worldpanel
Base: total music

Music Spend by Demographic Group

Under 20s account for a quarter of digital spend

The share of spend on music accounted for by women continues to fall – in 2009 it stood at 39.7% but dropped to 36.4% in 2010 and is now down to 35.7%. The decline is due principally to a drop in spend on physical albums, with two-year decreases experienced in both the artist and compilation CD markets. The percentage of expenditure attributable to women has varied in the digital music markets, declining in 2010 but rising again in 2011 in both the digital singles and albums sectors. Their share (44%) is still strongest in the compilations market but this has fallen, from 49.6% in 2009.

Buyers aged 35 to 44 are the key group in terms of overall spend, accounting for over a fifth (20.5%), but they are not top in every category. In compilations the 45 to 54 year olds edge them out narrowly, while in digital the largest share is attributable to the very youngest age group, rising to 29.0% in the singles market. The rise in importance of these youngest buyers has been swift – in 2009 they were responsible for 20.2% of digital music expenditure: this has now risen to 25.6%. It should be remembered, however, that this will commonly have taken place on a credit or debit card provided by parents.

Artist albums continue to attract a more predominantly male, affluent and slightly younger audience than compilations but it should be noted that Kantar's demographic data currently only covers physical purchases in both markets.

Music Spend by Demographic Group 2011 (% down)

		Total Music	All Albums	Physical Albums	Artist Albums	Compilation Albums	Total Digital Music	Digital Singles	Digital Albums
Gender	Female	35.7	36.2	38.0	36.9	44.0	30.7	33.0	29.1
	Male	64.3	63.8	62.0	63.1	56.0	69.3	67.0	70.9
Age Group	13-19	15.2	13.1	10.5	11.2	6.9	25.6	29.0	23.0
	20-24	9.2	7.9	6.6	6.5	6.9	15.0	17.8	12.9
	25-34	17.7	16.7	15.2	15.3	15.1	23.2	24.0	22.5
	35-44	20.5	21.4	22.5	22.4	23.0	16.2	14.5	17.5
	45-54	18.7	20.1	21.8	21.5	23.1	11.7	9.1	13.7
	55-64	11.7	13.0	14.4	14.1	15.7	5.9	3.6	7.7
	65-79	7.0	7.7	9.0	9.0	9.2	2.4	2.0	2.7
Social Group	AB	20.3	20.0	18.3	18.5	17.3	24.6	21.7	26.7
	C1	38.1	38.6	39.3	39.8	36.8	35.6	35.3	35.8
	C2	22.3	22.2	22.6	21.9	25.9	21.8	22.9	21.0
	DE	19.2	19.1	19.8	19.8	20.0	18.0	20.1	16.4

Source: Kantar Worldpanel

Music Spend by Lifestage Group

Families and older couples take largest shares in 2011

Children (respondents aged between 13 and 17) cumulatively spend the smallest amount on music of all the Lifestage groups but their share is growing – in 2009 it was 6.1% and is now 7.9%. Their influence is greatest in the singles market where they account for 16.0% of expenditure, although this was slightly down on 2010. Students' share of overall music spend has also improved over two years, with significant increases occurring in both the albums (from 7.8% in 2009 to 9.8% in 2011) and singles (from 14.8% to 21.3%) markets.

Spend by families has fluctuated, although their compilations share has now increased in two successive years and is still the market in which they are most important, accounting for 30.3%. Younger singles (those aged under 45) claim the biggest share in the singles market, their 22.4% edging out students' 21.3%. Older singles are by far the lowest spenders in the singles market, their largest share occurring in the Music DVD sector (17.1%), while older couples take a significant percentage in a number of markets, including physical music where they account for over a quarter of all spend. They are the second biggest spenders overall behind families.

Music Spend by Lifestage Group 2011 (% down)

	Total Music	All Albums	Physical Albums	Artist Albums	Compilation Albums	Total Digital Music	Digital Singles	Digital Albums
Children (Under 18)	7.9	6.7	5.7	6.1	3.7	12.7	16.0	10.3
Students	11.3	9.8	8.2	8.7	5.4	18.2	21.3	16.0
Families	22.8	23.4	24.1	22.9	30.3	19.8	18.6	20.7
Younger Singles (<45)	16.7	15.8	14.9	15.0	14.3	20.7	22.4	19.4
Younger Couples (<45)	10.6	10.6	9.9	10.2	8.2	12.4	10.9	13.5
Older Singles (45+)	9.6	10.5	11.8	11.8	11.8	4.9	3.8	5.7
Older Couples (45+)	21.0	23.1	25.4	25.2	26.3	11.4	7.1	14.5

Source: Kantar Worldpanel

Music Spend – Gender Profiles
Younger buyers taking larger share of women's spend

Music expenditure by women is becoming more heavily weighted towards younger buyers according to Kantar's data. From 2010 to 2011 all of the four older age groups saw their influence wane but the 13 to 19 year olds and the 25 to 34 year olds both took a larger share of spend, resulting in those two groups together representing over a third of female expenditure. That said, the key groups are still the 35 to 44 and 45 to 54 year olds, both accounting for 18.7%, with the latter responsible for one in every five albums bought in 2011. In the singles market the youngest group have greatest importance, representing well over a third (35.5%) of women's spend. Their influence is growing in terms of digital albums too – over a quarter (26.3%) of female spend is by the youngest consumers, up from 18.1% in 2009.

The 35 to 44 year olds are the most important group in terms of male expenditure, accounting for over a fifth of spend in the albums market and in terms of overall music spend by men as well. As with women, the youngest consumers are very important to the digital market, but while the 13 to 19 year olds are the biggest spenders on digital albums, the 25 to 34 year olds edge them in the singles market.

Buyers from the C1 social group remain the most important in terms of both male and female spend, representing over a third in all the categories presented here.

Female Expenditure by Age and Social Group 2011 (% down)

	Total Music	All Albums	Digital Singles	Digital Albums
13-19	16.4	13.7	35.5	26.3
20-24	8.5	7.3	17.2	11.1
25-34	17.5	17.2	19.5	27.9
35-44	18.7	19.6	12.0	13.4
45-54	18.7	20.1	8.2	11.0
55-64	12.0	13.1	4.6	6.7
65-79	8.2	9.0	3.1	3.6
AB	20.0	19.4	24.3	24.4
C1	38.3	38.8	35.1	35.8
C2	23.3	23.0	25.0	22.9
DE	18.4	18.7	15.7	16.8

Source: Kantar Worldpanel

Male Expenditure by Age and Social Group 2011 (% down)

	Total Music	All Albums	Digital Singles	Digital Albums
13-19	14.5	12.7	25.8	21.6
20-24	9.6	8.3	18.1	13.7
25-34	17.8	16.5	26.3	20.3
35-44	21.5	22.5	15.8	19.1
45-54	18.7	20.1	9.6	14.8
55-64	11.6	13.0	3.1	8.2
65-79	6.3	7.0	1.4	2.3
AB	20.4	20.4	20.5	27.7
C1	38.0	38.4	35.4	35.8
C2	21.8	21.8	21.9	20.2
DE	19.7	19.3	22.2	16.3

Source: Kantar Worldpanel

Penetration and Average Spend

Overall penetration falls again but average spend remains stable

Market penetration is a term used to describe the percentage of the population who have made at least one purchase in the previous 12 months. The top table looks at the levels across the different music markets from 2009 through 2011 and as can be seen, the percentage of people making any kind of musical purchase – physical or digital – fell again in 2011, to 47.8%. Levels have continued to fall in both the album and singles markets, with less than 40% of the population buying a physical album in 2011. The growing popularity of digital albums has, however, helped to ensure that an increased percentage (20.0%) of people bought some digital music in 2011. These figures would seem to suggest that new entrants to the digital market are confident enough to make album purchases straight away.

Average spend per buyer on music overall has remained relatively stable over this period but is decreasing in the albums market, with spend on CDs falling fairly swiftly. Spend per buyer on digital albums is now not far short of the per-consumer total for physical albums, quite a turnaround considering there was a £19 gulf between the two in 2009. The number of shoppers active in the singles market may be static according to Kantar, but they are increasing their spend – the per-buyer total has almost doubled in two years, from £9.85 to £17.09.

Penetration (%)

	2009	2010	2011
Total Music	52.8	49.1	47.8
All Albums	48.6	46.6	44.4
Singles	16.5	16.2	16.0
Physical Albums	46.2	43.2	39.4
Music DVD	6.2	5.9	4.7
Total Digital Music	18.2	19.5	20.0
Digital Albums	8.0	10.3	12.2

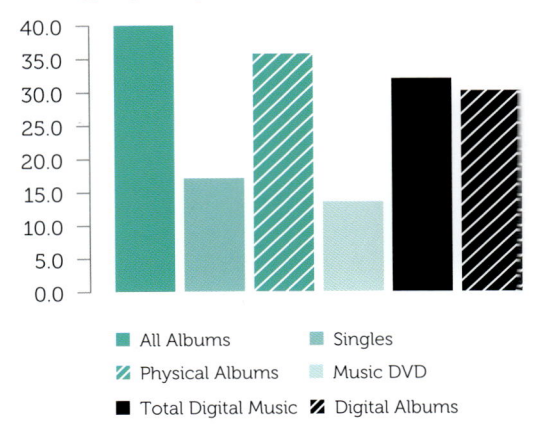

Source: Kantar Worldpanel

Average Spend per Buyer (£)

	2009	2010	2011
Total Music	£42.83	£42.87	£42.83
All Albums	£43.16	£40.73	£40.00
Singles	£9.85	£12.79	£17.09
Physical Albums	£41.50	£38.17	£35.70
Music DVD	£13.51	£13.45	£13.54
Total Digital Music	£18.23	£23.32	£32.02
Digital Albums	£22.52	£24.06	£30.17

Source: Kantar Worldpanel

Penetration – Total Market and Digital Music

Over a third of teens now buying digital music

Music purchasing numbers fell among both men and women in 2011 and only increased among the youngest of Kantar's survey respondents – 52.8% of 13 to 19 year olds bought at least one single or album, making them proportionally the second most active group. As in 2010, penetration levels are still above 50% in all but the two oldest groups, but both the 20 to 24 year olds and the 25 to 34s are close to slipping below that mark. Whereas the ABC1 buyers remained above that in 2010, this year all the social groups' penetration levels were below 50%, with AB consumers taking over as the most proportionally active.

More people are buying digital music overall than they were in 2010, but the increase was only marginal among men. Although more people in the three youngest age groups are now buying digital music, penetration is falling among the key 35 to 54 groups. However, the decreases are small and they are not necessarily representative of longer term trends.

The 45 to 54 age group still had the highest percentage of physical album purchasers in 2011 but it has dropped from 50.9% in 2009 to 45.6% in 2011.

Penetration by Gender, Age and Social Group – Total Music (%)

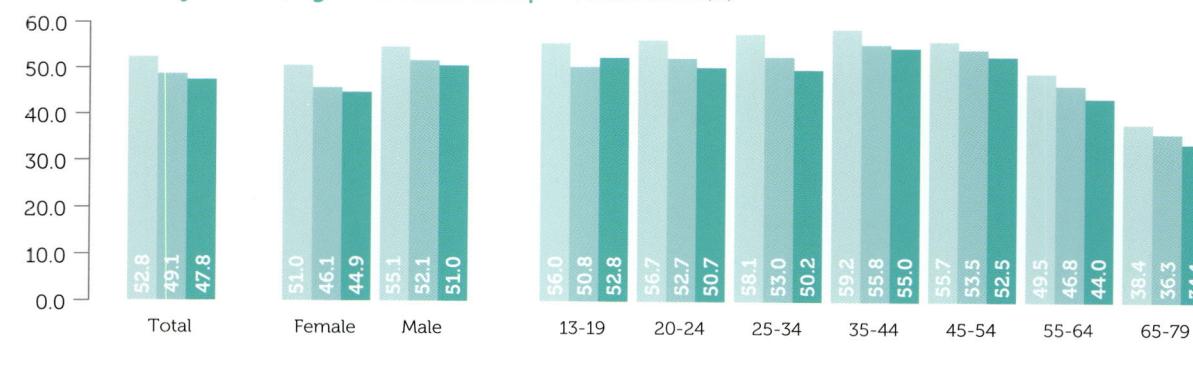

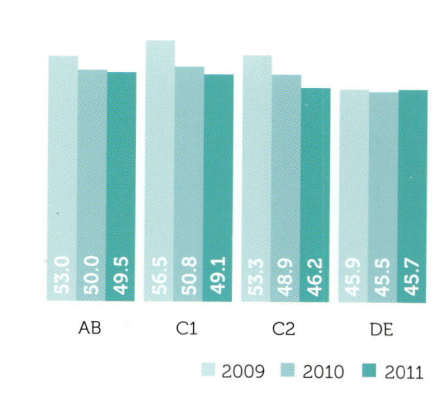

	Total	Female	Male	13-19	20-24	25-34	35-44	45-54	55-64	65-79	AB	C1	C2	DE
2009	52.8	51.0	55.1	56.0	56.7	58.1	59.2	55.7	49.5	38.4	53.0	56.5	53.3	45.9
2010	49.1	46.1	52.1	50.8	52.7	53.0	55.8	53.5	46.8	36.3	50.0	50.8	48.9	45.5
2011	47.8	44.9	51.0	52.8	50.7	50.2	55.0	52.5	44.0	34.1	49.5	49.1	46.2	45.7

Penetration by Gender, Age and Social Group – Digital Music (%)

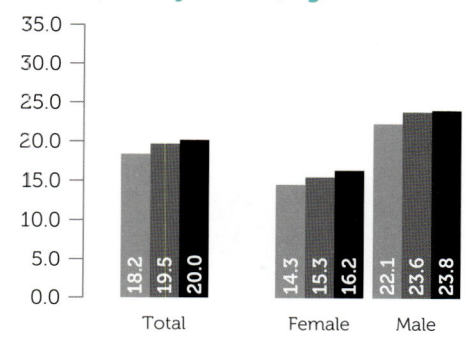

	Total	Female	Male	13-19	20-24	25-34	35-44	45-54	55-64	65-79	AB	C1	C2	DE
2009	18.2	14.3	22.1	30.3	28.8	27.5	23.2	15.4	9.3	5.2	20.3	19.8	17.8	13.7
2010	19.5	15.3	23.6	30.1	30.7	28.3	24.5	16.4	11.1	6.1	21.8	20.2	19.0	16.8
2011	20.0	16.2	23.8	34.0	32.5	28.8	24.0	16.3	10.3	5.3	23.4	20.2	19.4	16.9

Source: Kantar Worldpanel

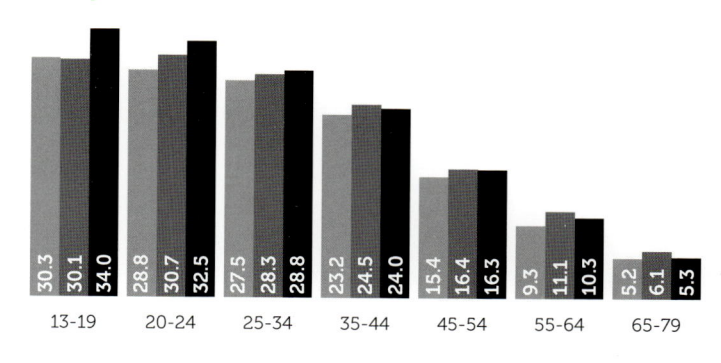

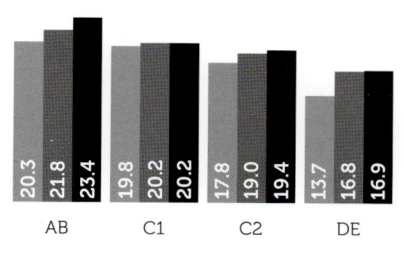

Average Spend – Total Market and Digital Music

Digital spend per buyer increases in every age group

The average amount spent per music buyer has remained relatively stable for the past three years, but the decreasing number of people making purchases is driving retail sales down. As the top chart shows, overall spend is only marginally down and has actually increased in four of the seven age groups. It should be noted, however, that average expenditure per buyer fell quite sharply among 45 to 54 year olds, who are currently the second biggest spending group. Also of some concern is that average spend by women has decreased in two successive years – in 2009 it stood at £34.56 but is now down to £32.53. Their spend has decreased significantly on physical albums, dropping from £33.82 in 2009 to £27.29 in 2011.

Average spend per buyer on digital music has risen by over a third from 2010 to 2011, increasing by a significant amount among both women and men and across every age group. Buyers aged 13 to 19 have significantly increased their individual spend between 2009 and 2011 and this group spends the most per buyer in both the digital singles and albums markets. In the singles market average spend decreases as the buying groups get older but in the digital albums sector two of the oldest groups (the 45 to 54 and 55 to 64 year olds) are among the highest average spenders.

Average Spend per Buyer within Gender, Age and Social Group – Total Music (£)

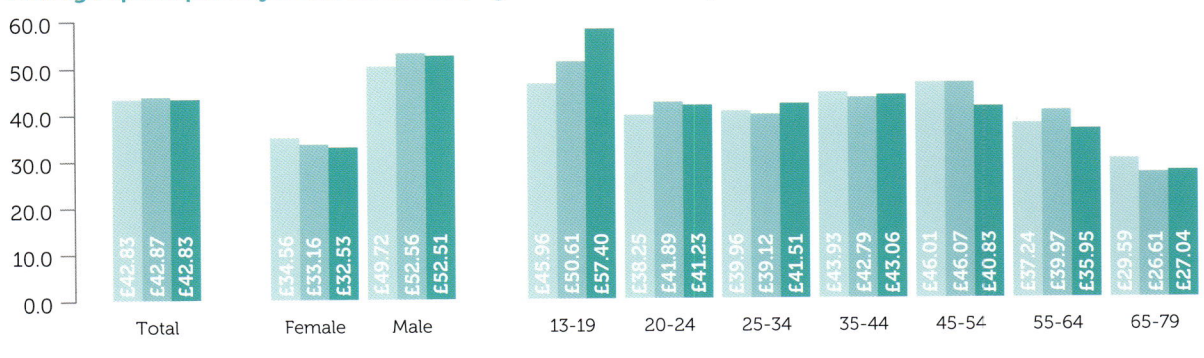

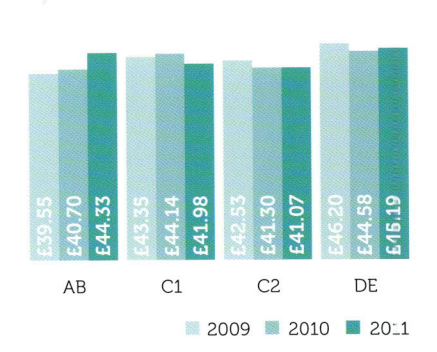

Group	2009	2010	2011
Total	£42.83	£42.87	£42.83
Female	£34.56	£33.16	£32.53
Male	£49.72	£52.56	£52.51
13-19	£45.96	£50.61	£57.40
20-24	£38.25	£41.89	£41.23
25-34	£39.96	£39.12	£41.51
35-44	£43.93	£42.79	£43.06
45-54	£46.01	£46.07	£40.83
55-64	£37.24	£39.97	£35.95
65-79	£29.59	£26.61	£27.04
AB	£39.55	£40.70	£44.33
C1	£43.35	£44.14	£41.98
C2	£42.53	£41.30	£41.07
DE	£46.20	£44.58	£46.19

Average Spend per Buyer within Gender, Age and Social Group – Digital Music (£)

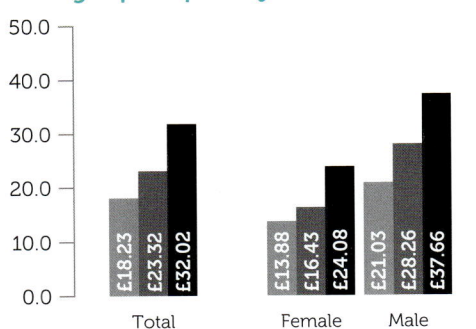

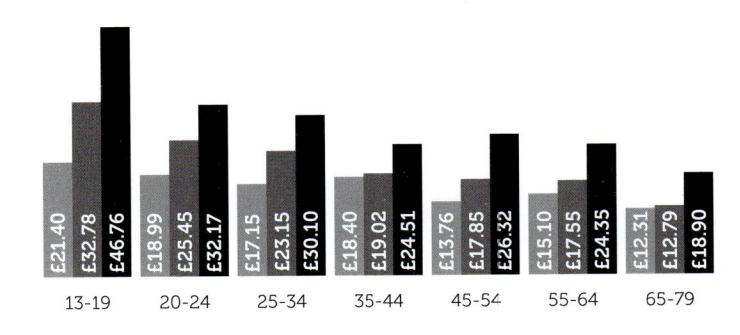

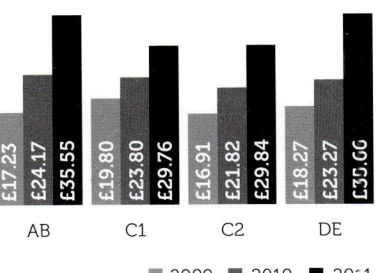

Group	2009	2010	2011
Total	£18.23	£23.32	£32.02
Female	£13.88	£16.43	£24.08
Male	£21.03	£28.26	£37.66
13-19	£21.40	£32.78	£46.76
20-24	£18.99	£25.45	£32.17
25-34	£17.15	£23.15	£30.10
35-44	£18.40	£19.02	£24.51
45-54	£13.76	£17.85	£26.32
55-64	£15.10	£17.55	£24.35
65-79	£12.31	£12.79	£18.90
AB	£17.23	£24.17	£35.55
C1	£19.80	£23.80	£29.76
C2	£16.91	£21.82	£29.84
DE	£18.27	£23.27	£35.06

Source: Kantar Worldpanel

CONSUMER DATA

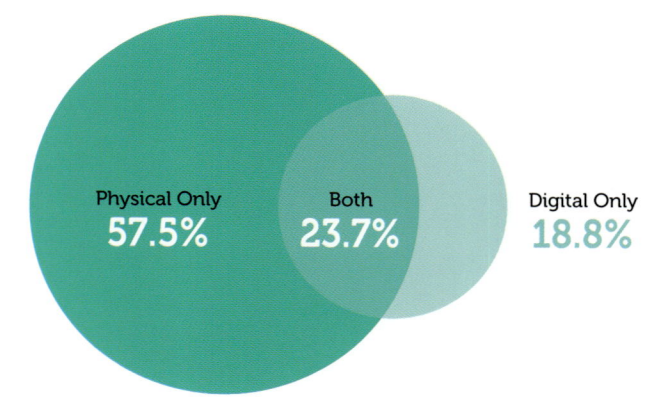

Digital/Physical Crossover of Music Buyers – Share
Physical-only buyers account for greatest share of expenditure

While those who purchase only physical music are still in the majority, they constituted a slightly diminished share (57.5%) of the music buying population in 2011. The proportion of consumers now buying only digital music edged closer to a fifth (18.8%) while the percentage of those buying both physical and digital music declined to 23.7%.

The stacked bar chart shows the percentage of spend in the different music markets that each of the three buying groups accounted for in 2011. Those buyers only purchasing music on physical formats are still hugely important, their spend comprising 45.7% of all music expenditure, rising to over half (52.7%) in the albums market. Digital-only buyers account for the majority of expenditure on singles but are edged out by 'crossover' buyers (i.e. those who purchase both physical and digital music) in the digital albums sector.

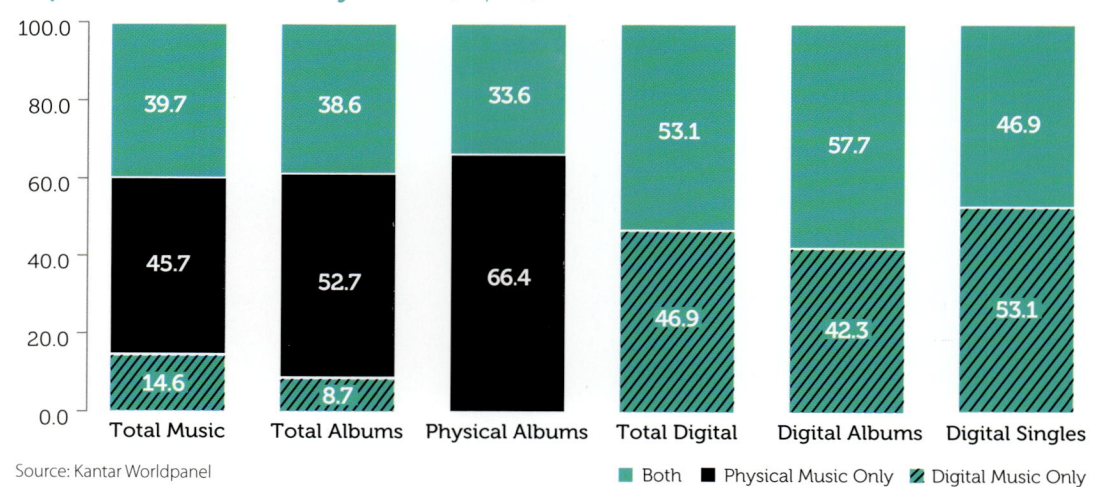

Importance of Crossover Buyers 2011 (% spend)

	Both	Physical Music Only	Digital Music Only
Total Music	39.7	45.7	14.6
Total Albums	38.6	52.7	8.7
Physical Albums	33.6	66.4	—
Total Digital	53.1	—	46.9
Digital Albums	57.7	—	42.3
Digital Singles	46.9	—	53.1

Source: Kantar Worldpanel

Crossover of Music Buyers (%)

	2010	2011
Digital Music Only	17.2	18.8
Physical Music Only	58.5	57.5
Both	24.3	23.7

Source: Kantar Worldpanel

Crossover of Music Buyers 2011 (%)

Physical Only **57.5%** — Both **23.7%** — Digital Only **18.8%**

Source: Kantar Worldpanel

Digital/Physical Crossover of Music Buyers – Demographics

Teens account for a fifth of all digital-only buyers

The top chart on this page looks at age profile by format preference. The physical-only demographic is weighted towards older buyers, as might be expected, with those aged over 45 accounting for over half (55.4%) of the consumers active in this market. This is also a sector slightly weighted towards female buyers – as can be seen on page 80 their penetration level in the digital music market lags behind men. Buyers aged 25 to 34 make up the biggest of the 'digital only' age groups as well as constituting the biggest proportion of crossover purchasers. Men make up the greater share in both of these groups.

Data from Kantar also shows that purchasers buying both physical and digital music in 2011 spent over twice as much as consumers that restricted their buying to just one or the other. Crossover buyers spent an average of £67.85 on music, compared to £32.14 for physical only buyers, and £31.57 for those only purchasing digital music.

Crossover of Music Buyers – Age and Gender Breakdown (% buyers)

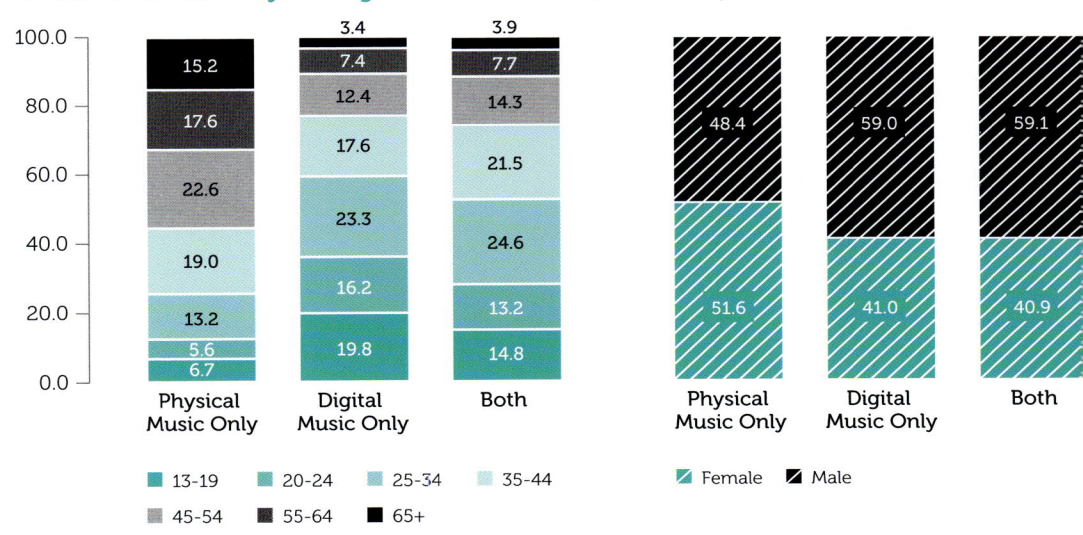

Age	Physical Music Only	Digital Music Only	Both
13-19	6.7	19.8	14.8
20-24	5.6	16.2	13.2
25-34	13.2	23.3	24.6
35-44	19.0	17.6	21.5
45-54	22.6	12.4	14.3
55-64	17.6	7.4	7.7
65+	15.2	3.4	3.9

Gender	Physical Music Only	Digital Music Only	Both
Female	51.6	41.0	40.9
Male	48.4	59.0	59.1

Source: Kantar Worldpanel

Average Spend per Buyer 2011 (£)

- Digital only: £31.57
- Physical only: £32.14
- Both: £67.85

Source: Kantar Worldpanel

CONSUMER DATA

83

Decile Analysis and Spend Composition

Heaviest 10% of buyers account for 45% of music spend

The top table on this page looks at how expenditure in the different markets is concentrated towards the most active buyers. For instance, it can be seen that the top spending 10% of buyers in the overall music market account for 45.1% of the expenditure total in 2011, but in the singles market the first decile's spend represents over half (53.1%). In fact the biggest spending 30% of singles buyers are responsible for a huge proportion (83.3%), even if this percentage is slightly down on 2010's 86.9%. The key observation, however, is how important the biggest spenders are right across the board – they account for at least 44% in every category.

Although Kantar's data cannot list out digital compilation and artist album purchases separately, it is possible to look at the proportion of spend the four main product categories make up across the demographic groups. Compilations actually comprise a greater proportion of women's spend than men's but their lower spend overall means that men take a greater share of expenditure in this market (see page 76). Physical albums make up almost 90% of spend by the oldest buyers and compilation CDs represent less than 10% of spend by the most affluent social group, the AB buyers.

Spend by Buyer Decile 2011 (% down)

	Total Music	Physical Music	Digital Music	Albums	Singles
Top 10%	45.1	45.2	48.0	44.9	53.1
11-20%	18.2	16.5	20.5	17.4	19.4
21-30%	11.2	10.8	11.7	10.9	10.8
31-40%	7.9	8.0	7.2	7.9	6.4
41-50%	5.7	5.7	4.8	5.8	4.1
51-60%	4.2	4.4	3.2	4.3	2.7
61-70%	3.1	4.0	2.2	3.4	1.5
71-100%	4.6	5.5	2.4	5.4	2.0

Source: Kantar Worldpanel

Spend Composition by Gender 2011 (%)

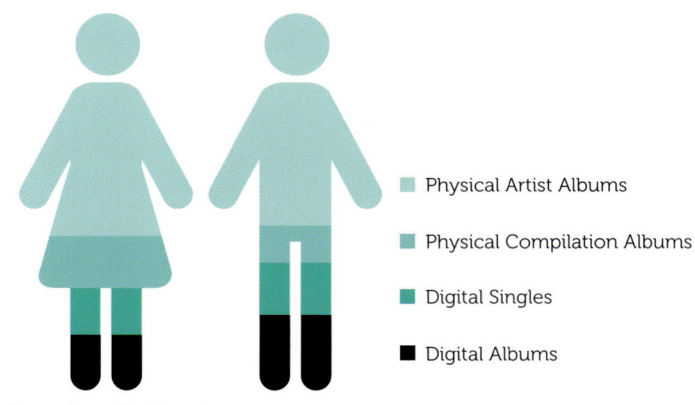

- Physical Artist Albums
- Physical Compilation Albums
- Digital Singles
- Digital Albums

Source: Kantar Worldpanel

Spend Composition by Gender, Age and Social Group 2011

(% down)	Women	Men	13-19	20-24	25-34	35-44	45-54	55-64	65-79	AB	C1	C2	DE
Physical Artist Albums	59.4	56.6	42.3	40.8	49.6	62.8	66.5	69.2	74.5	52.5	60.1	56.5	59.2
Physical Compilation Albums	13.7	9.7	5.1	8.4	9.5	12.5	13.8	15.0	14.8	9.5	10.8	13.0	11.6
Digital Singles	12.3	13.9	25.5	25.7	18.1	9.4	6.5	4.0	3.7	14.3	12.3	13.7	13.9
Digital Albums	14.6	19.8	27.1	25.1	22.8	15.3	13.2	11.8	6.9	23.7	16.8	16.8	15.3

Source: Kantar Worldpanel

Demographic Case Study – Adele's *21*
One in every seven households buys a copy in 2011

The sheer volume in which **Adele**'s *21* was bought gives rise to some interesting statistics. Not only is it, at the time of writing, the sixth biggest-selling album of all time (recently overtaking **Pink Floyd**'s ***Dark Side Of The Moon*** and **Dire Straits**' ***Brothers In Arms***) but, in 2011, it found its way into one in every seven households in the UK.

Its popularity seems to have mobilised a significant number of lapsed music buyers to make a purchase. According to Kantar's data – which tracks the purchasing behaviour of its respondents over time – 12.5% of those who bought *21* did not buy any other albums in 2011, and 18.6% did not purchase an album in 2010. Over a quarter of those who bought it were classed as 'light' buyers, which Kantar defines as anyone spending less than £22.97 on music in a single year.

While men accounted for 63.8% of spend on albums in 2011, the balance was somewhat different for this title, with women responsible for over half of spend. The core age groups (25 through to 54) remained the same as in the wider albums market, with *21*'s audience demographic less weighted towards those aged over 55. There were no significant differences in the social make-up of its audience, with the share of expenditure following the same order.

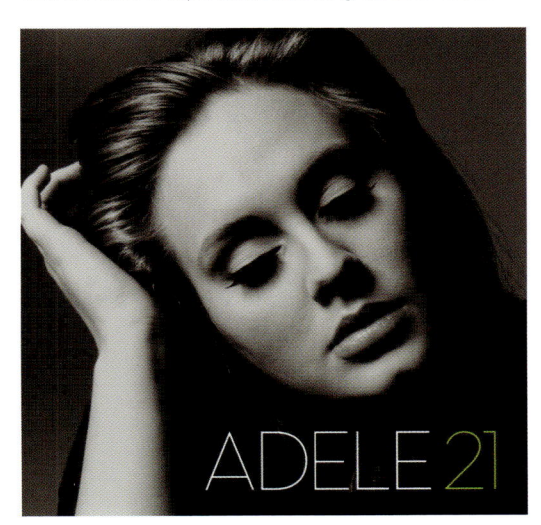

Buyers by Consumption Category
(% buyers, down)

Heavy	(more than £67.20)	33.3
Medium	(£22.98 to £67.20)	41.2
Light	(less than £22.97)	25.6

Source: Kantar Worldpanel

Demographic Profile of '21' Buyers
(% spend, down)

Under 20	13.7
20-24	6.7
25-34	20.9
35-44	22.8
45-54	22.0
55-64	11.0
65-79	2.9
Female	51.5
Male	48.5
AB	18.5
C1	38.1
C2	24.4
DE	19.0
No Children	62.8
1 Child	19.8
2 Children	13.1
3+ Children	4.4

Source: Kantar Worldpanel

Music Consumption

Smartphones and tablets drive listening 'on the go'

The methods by which people acquire, store and listen to music are evolving all the time. In the albums market the CD is still king, accounting for over three quarters of all purchases in 2011. The near-ubiquity of broadband (which is now accessed by three quarters of UK households) and comprehensive 3G coverage however has meant that online music is easily within reach both at home and on the move. While the continued growth of a la carte downloading has shown that the desire to own music is still very strong, streaming services are becoming firmly mainstream. Data from Nielsen shows YouTube's UK audience topped 20m in the last two months of 2011 while Spotify hit the 3m paying subscriber mark globally in January 2012.

MUSIC ON MOBILE

The facility to cache tracks on a mobile has now become a standard feature of most music subscription services, meaning that non-owned tracks and albums can be accessed anywhere, even when there is no signal. This is not to say however that a la carte downloading on mobiles is no longer a significant part of the digital music offer – mobile accounted for 50% of tracks downloaded globally from the service 7digital in 2011. Take-up has been driven by applications being pre-loaded onto devices as well as updated apps on the Android and Blackberry platforms.

As Futuresource's data shows (see table), smartphones are now owned by over half of the UK population, and they forecast penetration to rise to around two thirds this year. Standalone MP3 players are owned by over a quarter of people and tablets are now gaining a foothold, with Futuresource estimating that over 5m will be sold in 2012. Data from Nielsen found that in the final quarter of 2011 19% of tablet owners paid for music through their device – while this is some way off the 62% recorded in the US, clearly the scope for accessing music on the move has never been greater.

IN-HOME LISTENING

Methods of listening to music at home are also diversifying. Ownership of home audio systems may be dropping slightly overall but there is growing interest in networked listening. Dedicated streaming audio hardware firms (such as Sonos) are partnering with music services and more and more listeners are wirelessly linking up their computers and phones to their systems. Another further avenue for growth is that of access through console gaming – Microsoft said in February 2012 that owners signed up to the Xbox Live online service now spend an average of 84 hours a month on it, with over half of that time dedicated to watching videos and listening to music rather than gaming. Sony's PS3 also offers music videos and streaming audio through its online portal and its Music Unlimited service can be accessed through internet-enabled TV sets as well. Ipsos Media CT's Technology Tracker from the third quarter of 2011 found that 16% of UK adults are now accessing the internet through a TV, in most cases via a games console.

Key Metrics

	2010	2011	2012*
Broadband household connections (m)	19.0	19.6	20.3
Household penetration	72%	74%	76%
Typical achieved broadband download speed (mbps)	5.4	7.0	8.8
Home audio hardware installed base (m)**	26.6	25.8	24.7
% networked	2%	5%	9%
Total MP3 player installed base (m)	17.4	16.6	14.9
Personal penetration	28%	27%	24%
Smartphones in use (m)	27.8	35.3	42.9
Personal penetration	45%	57%	68%
Tablets installed base (m)	1.4	3.5	5.5
Household penetration	2%	7%	15%

Source: Futuresource Consulting
*forecast
**Includes integrated audio systems, dedicated speaker docks and networked speakers, A/V receivers, HTiB and pure soundbars

RADIO AND PATTERNS OF ACCESSING MUSIC

Radio remains a central part of the nation's listening habits. Just under 90% of the population listened every week in 2011 according to RAJAR, with over 23m doing so digitally, via either a DAB set, through the TV or the internet – equivalent to 29% of all radio listening in the final quarter of the year.

Another wave of Harris Interactive's Fast Forward survey was undertaken in August and provides an interesting snapshot of people's music listening patterns. Over a third of their online respondents (37%) stated that they streamed music from social networks at least monthly and over half (58%) stated that they watch videos every month on YouTube. A significant proportion (29%) listen to music stored on their mobiles and 11% use their phones to watch music videos, a similar percentage to those who listen to streamed music (10%). These activities increase significantly among the younger respondents – 52% of 16 to 24 year olds listen to music stored on the device, with a third (32%) from that age group watching music videos and a quarter (24%) listening to streamed music.

While YouTube's statistics dwarf those of other streaming services, it should be remembered that this is both a free-to-access channel and that not all of its content is music-related. Vevo only officially launched in April 2011 in the UK but by the beginning of 2012 was reporting nearly 12m unique visitors every month, with an average of 15 videos viewed per user per month. There are also some encouraging signs in the a la carte downloading market: as the Consumer Data chapter in this book shows, music was downloaded legally by a fifth of the population in 2011.

UNAUTHORISED SERVICES

Levels of piracy in the UK, however, show few signs of abating. According to data from UKOM/Nielsen, who monitor actual website and application usage, around 7m people in the UK were frequenting at least one unauthorised service in 2011. There were as many as 4.3m P2P users in any one month, including as many as 2m using the uTorrent application alone. Around 2m visited locker sites on a regular basis, and when stream rippers, forums, overseas paysites and blog aggregators are factored in the total rises to almost 4m across non-P2P sites and services. All feed into the wider spectrum of unauthorised activity that continues to challenge growth and innovation – while it remains unchecked it will be increasingly difficult for the services licensing music legally to flourish.

Music Services – Monthly Activity (% using)

Listen to DAB radio	43%
Stream music from social networks	37%
Listen to music stored on mobile	29%
Watch music videos on mobile	11%
Listen to streamed music via mobile	10%

Source: Harris Interactive Fast Forward (Aug 2011)

Pirate Sites and Applications – Unique Users per Month 2011 (millions)

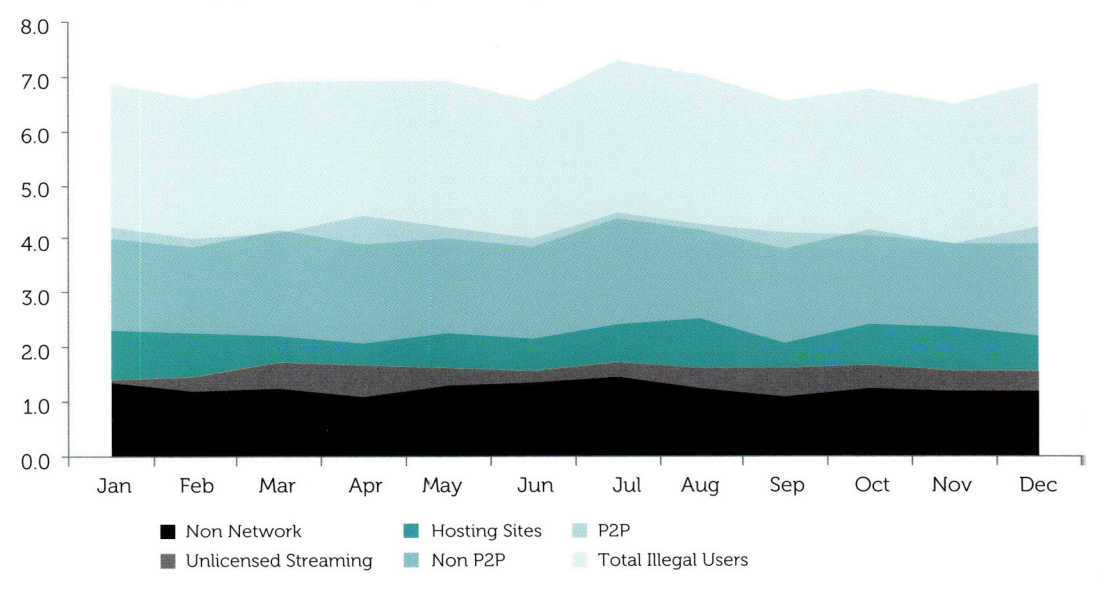

Source: Nielsen/UKOM

World Sales

UK market decline in step with global revenues in 2011

The decline in trade revenues of 3.0% in 2011 was a much smaller downturn than recorded in 2010, when global industry income fell by 8.4%. IFPI's market measurement includes public performance and synchronisation income, both of which grew in 2011 and together with a growing digital business helped to offset most of the 8.7% drop in physical format sales.

Synchronisation income captures record company's earnings from licensing recordings for use in films, adverts and games. The addition of 'sync' income is a welcome addition to the presentation of market data and helps to illustrate how the industry's revenue streams are diversifying in the 21st century. In 2011 the sync market was valued at US$342m by IFPI, 2% of global recorded music sales.

The total market value fell to US$16.6 billion but the main success story of the year was once again the growth of digital, which increased by 8.0% and now accounts for 31% of overall music revenues around the world although, as shown on the following page, this varies substantially from territory to territory.

Germany retained its position as the third largest market in the world, whilst the UK remained in fourth place with its market decline in line with the overall downturn. There were, however, several territories where revenues increased including Canada (+2.6%), Sweden (+3.0%), South Korea (+6.4%), Brazil (+8.6%) and Australia (+5.7%). With the US and German markets being flat in 2011, the outlook for the industry in terms of growth is probably a little better than it has been for some time, especially as meaningful measures are being put in place in several countries to deal with the ongoing problems caused by the illegal online distribution of music.

Worldwide Recorded Music Trade Revenues 2011 (US$m)

	2010	2011	% change
Physical formats	11,142	10,170	-8.7%
Digital	4,840	5,229	8.0%
Performance rights	862	905	5.0%
Synchronisation	324	342	5.6%
Total	17,168	16,646	-3.0%

Source: IFPI

Top 10 International Markets 2011

		Market Value (trade income US$m)	% change from 2010	Share of Global Revenues
1	USA	4,372.9	-0.1%	26.3%
2	Japan	4,087.7	-7.0%	24.6%
3	Germany	1,473.7	-0.2%	8.9%
4	UK	1,433.7	-3.1%	8.6%
5	France	1,002.2	-3.7%	6.0%
6	Australia	475.2	5.7%	2.9%
7	Canada	434.0	2.6%	2.6%
8	Brazil	262.6	8.6%	1.6%
9	Netherlands	240.2	-12.1%	1.4%
10	Italy	239.9	-6.4%	1.4%

Source: IFPI

Breakdown of World Sales 2011

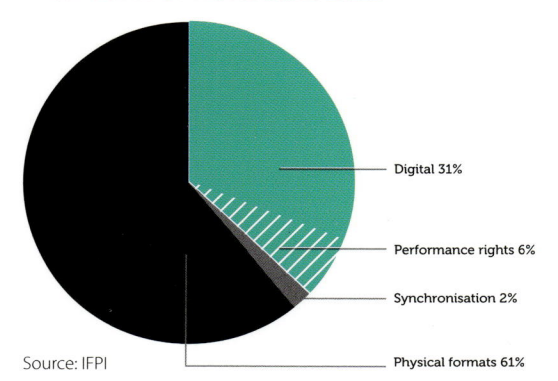

- Digital 31%
- Performance rights 6%
- Synchronisation 2%
- Physical formats 61%

Source: IFPI

The International Market for Digital Music

Almost a third of industry revenue now accounted for by digital

As the first graph shows, the increase in digital music's share of global industry revenues has been growing consistently and in 2011 it accounted for 31% of industry turnover, more than trebling since 2006.

When digital's share is examined on a country by country basis, the differences are vast as the second graph shows. Only the world's top 15 territories are represented here, but there are several others with large digital shares. In China and Thailand digital accounts for more than 70% of revenues whilst Malaysia, India and Indonesia all have digital shares of 60% or more.

The UK has the most advanced digital music market in Europe. There are more than 70 licensed services offering the consumer a variety of different ways to access music either to own or to stream. Only the Scandinavian territories of Sweden, Norway and Denmark have larger digital shares than the UK, claiming 53%, 41% and 38% respectively. Streaming subscriptions have demonstrated particularly strong growth in this region. In Sweden for example Spotify accounts for around 80% of digital revenues.

With recent developments around the world, the outlook for further digital growth looks positive. Here are a few key developments from 2011:

* IFPI's digital service tracking shows that the biggest digital music services are now present in 58 markets
* Apple's iTunes service opened in another 28 markets in 2011 including 16 Latin American territories. It is now operational in all EU countries
* Amid much media coverage, Spotify launched in the US as well as four more European countries in 2011 and now has a consumer offer in 12 countries
* Deezer's ambitious launch programme continued in 2011. It is now available in 25 countries in Europe and has announced extensive expansion plans for 2012
* Sony's Music Unlimited service is now live in 13 countries
* One development which is sure to attract a lot of media attention in 2012 is the expected expansion of Google's music service which was unveiled towards the end of 2011 in the USA

Digital's Share of Global Industry Revenue

Year	Share
2006	10.0%
2007	15.0%
2008	21.0%
2009	25.0%
2010	28.0%
2011	31.0%

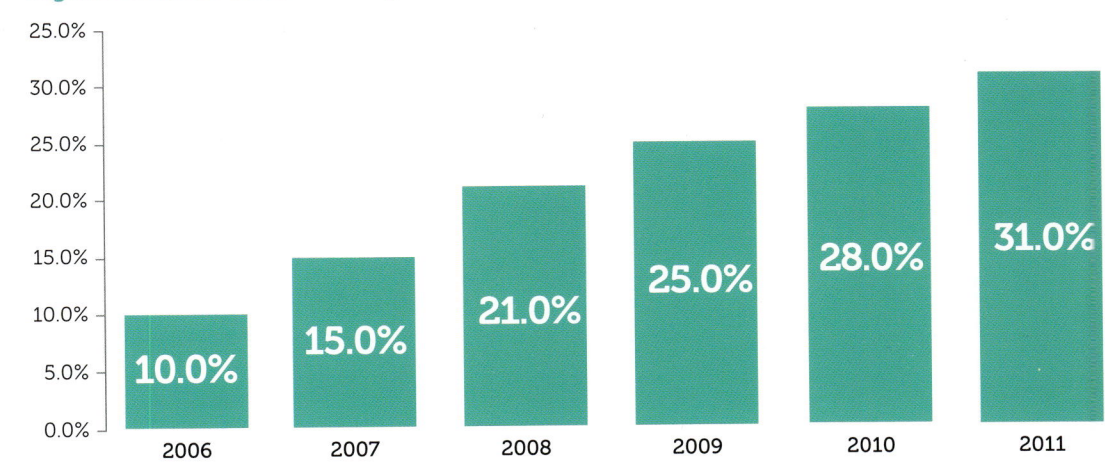

Source: IFPI

Digital's Share of Industry Revenue by Country 2011 – Top 15 International Markets

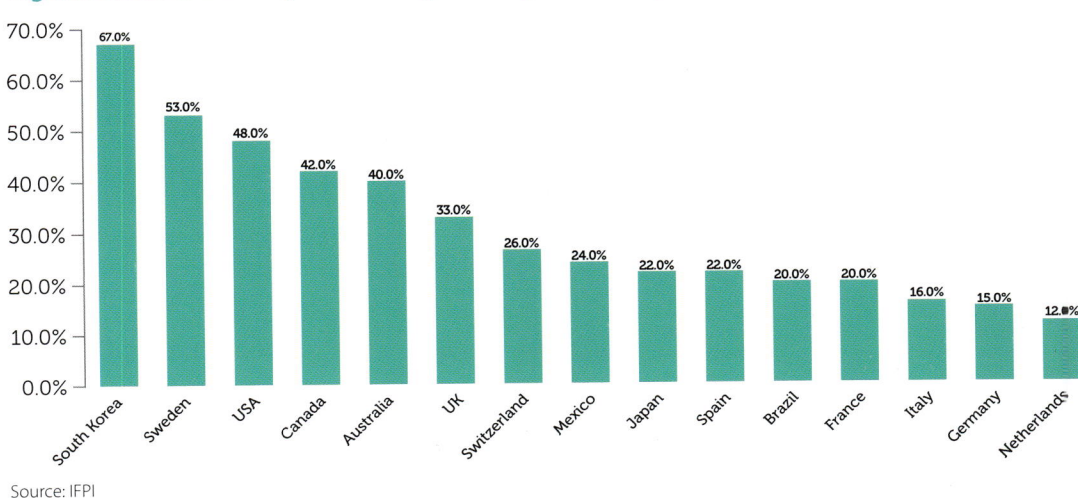

Country	Share
South Korea	67.0%
Sweden	53.0%
USA	48.0%
Canada	42.0%
Australia	40.0%
UK	33.0%
Switzerland	26.0%
Mexico	24.0%
Japan	22.0%
Spain	22.0%
Brazil	20.0%
France	20.0%
Italy	16.0%
Germany	15.0%
Netherlands	12.0%

Source: IFPI

UK Music in the International Market
Adele breaks records around the world as *21* tops annual chart

For the fourth time in the past five years, a British performer was responsible for the best selling artist album around the world in 2011. **Adele** followed **Amy Winehouse** (*Back To Black* in 2007), **Coldplay** (*Viva La Vida*, 2008) and **Susan Boyle** (*I Dreamed A Dream*, 2009).

This extraordinary run of success underlines the ongoing achievements of UK artists and record companies in overseas markets and the appeal that British music has around the world. In 2011, no fewer than nine of the top 50 global best sellers were by British artists – an export performance to be proud of.

BPI analysis of international sales charts showed that in 2011 UK artists accounted for 12.6% of artist albums sold around the world. This was an improvement on the already-impressive share of 11.8% claimed in 2010.

Last year undoubtedly belonged to **Adele** – her second album sold more than 18m copies across the globe making it the biggest selling album of the past 10 years. Her debut album *19* received a substantial sales boost and was the overall sixth biggest seller of the year, enjoying high chart positions around the world, three years after its original release.

Appearing in this chart for the third consecutive year with different albums was **Susan Boyle**. *Someone To Watch Over Me* was the sixth best seller by a British artist, despite only being released in November. It made a significant impression in several territories with top 10 placings in Australia, USA, Canada, Sweden, Belgium and of course the UK.

Florence & The Machine featured in the top 10 for a second year. *Lungs* was the fifth best selling UK album in 2010 and also made the top 10 in 2011. Her second album *Ceremonials* also featured at number nine, selling well throughout the world and topping the chart in Australia, New Zealand, UK and Ireland.

Amy Winehouse's collection *Lioness: Hidden Treasures* was the eleventh best selling album of the year and her untimely passing also meant that *Back To Black* featured in the annual chart for the third time in the past five years.

INDUSTRY REVENUE PER CAPITA 2011

UK music consumers have consistently been amongst the highest spending in the world and analysis in IFPI's Recording Industry In Numbers 2012 shows that this is still the case. In 2011 only Japan and Norway generated more revenue per head of the population than the UK. All but one of the top 10 territories in this analysis are European. Average revenue per capita in the USA was US$14.0, around two thirds that of the UK.

Best Selling Albums by British Artists Worldwide 2011

	Overall	Artist	Title	Company
1	1	Adele	*21*	XL Recordings
2	4	Coldplay	*Mylo Xyloto*	EMI Music
3	6	Adele	*19*	XL Recordings
4	11	Amy Winehouse	*Lioness: Hidden Treasures*	Universal Music
5	13	Mumford & Sons	*Sigh No More*	Universal Music/Glassnote Records/Sony Music
6	20	Susan Boyle	*Someone To Watch Over Me*	Sony Music
7	26	Jessie J	*Who You Are*	Universal Music
8	28	Amy Winehouse	*Back To Black*	Universal Music
9	37	Florence & The Machine	*Ceremonials*	Universal Music
10	57	Florence & The Machine	*Lungs*	Universal Music

Source: IFPI

Top 10 Markets by Revenue per Capita 2011

	Market Value (US$m)	Population (m)	Revenue per capita
Japan	4,087.7	126.5	$32.31
Norway	115.1	4.7	$24.49
UK	1,433.7	62.7	$22.87
Australia	475.2	21.8	$21.80
Switzerland	158.3	7.8	$20.29
Denmark	100.6	5.5	$18.29
Germany	1,473.7	81.5	$18.08
Sweden	155.3	9.5	$16.35
France	1,002.2	65.3	$15.35
Austria	118.9	8.2	$14.50

Source: IFPI

UK Music in Germany & France

Impressive shares recorded by UK artists in both France & Germany in 2011

Adele's **21** was the best selling album in both Germany and France in 2011. Yet despite outselling the nearest rival by more than three to one in Germany, UK artists' share of sales fell slightly to 16.4% and was overtaken by their share of the French market, which rose to 17.0%.

Data from IFPI shows that Germany and France were the third and fifth most important markets in the world in 2011 accounting for 9% and 6% of global sales values respectively.

MIXED RESULTS FOR UK ARTIST SHARE IN GERMANY & FRANCE

The German market has always been receptive to British music and a healthy share of sales was again recorded in 2011, with one in six albums sold accounted for by British artists. Yet despite this and the sales achievements of **Adele**, UK artists' share of sales fell by 1.5 percentage points to 16.4%. This is illustrated by the fact that there were fewer UK artists among the best sellers in Germany in 2011 – in 2010 18 of the top 100 albums were by UK acts compared to only 10 in 2011.

In France, however, share grew by 2.5 percentage points to 17.0%. There were a similar number of British artists among the best sellers, but share was boosted by **Adele – 21** outsold its nearest rival by almost four to one.

These statistics underline the UK industry's long-standing record of export achievement. This is well illustrated by the fact that last year German and French acts accounted for 0.9% and 0.3% of artist album sales in the UK respectively.

MARKET DIFFERENTIALS

Unusually, the top three albums by British artists were the same in Germany and France in 2011. Outside of the top five or six albums in each territory though there were large differences in the levels of success across some albums. There are many whose popularity in one territory is more marked than in others. Examples of this include the success of **Seal**, **Charlie Winston** and **Jamiroquai** in France or **Take That**, **Joe Cocker** and **Depeche Mode** in Germany.

Amy MacDonald has been one of the leading UK artists in Germany for a few years now and **A Curious Thing**, originally released in 2009 made the top 50 best selling albums in 2011.

Sales have been sustained by the release of an orchestral version which contains an extra disc of live recordings made with the **German Philharmonic Orchestra**. In France, though, the album featured at 550 in the annual chart.

Another example of the market differences is **Seal** – last year in France he accounted for five of the UK's 165 albums in the top 1,000, with **Soul II** being the fifth biggest selling British album and the 30th overall. Sales in the German market were at a lower level, with no titles featuring in the annual chart.

CHART ACHIEVEMENTS

The table shows the number of albums by British artists featuring in the annual top 1,000 albums in each of the two territories featured on this page. With the exception of France in 2008, UK artists have consistently accounted for around 150-180 of the best-selling titles in each country in the past four years, a significant achievement that illustrates the breadth and depth of UK repertoire.

British Artists' Chart Achievements

Number of Titles in Year End:	Germany 2009	Germany 2010	Germany 2011	France 2009	France 2010	France 2011
Top 10	3	1	1	3	1	2
Top 100	16	18	11	15	15	12
Top 500	87	99	87	77	77	80
Top 1,000	177	186	173	152	167	165

Source: BPI based on Media Control GfK data

UK Artists Share of Album Sales in Germany & France

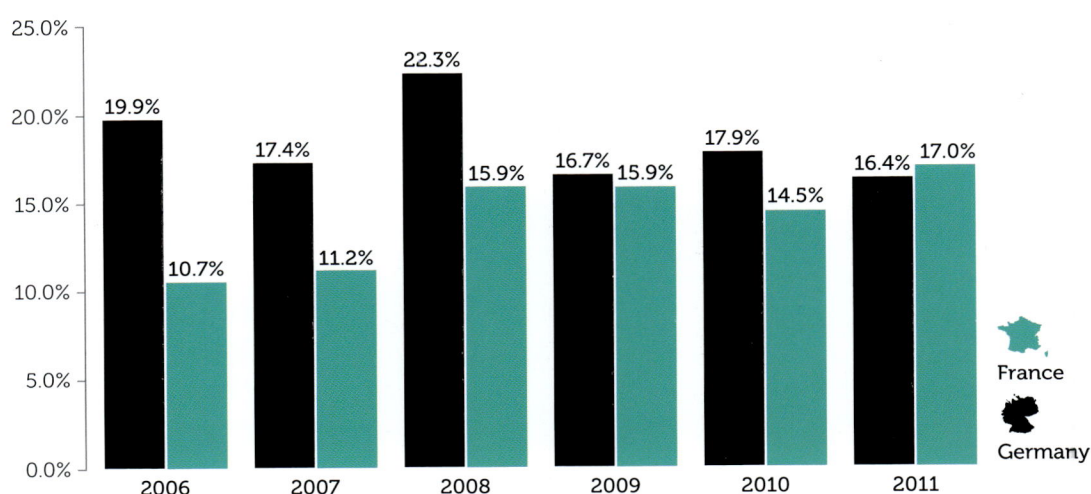

Year	Germany	France
2006	19.9%	10.7%
2007	17.4%	11.2%
2008	22.3%	15.9%
2009	16.7%	15.9%
2010	17.9%	14.5%
2011	16.4%	17.0%

Source: BPI based on Media Control GfK data

UK Music in North America
Grammy success rounds off incredible 12 months for Adele

Adele's phenomenal global success in 2011 has boosted the share of British music around the world. This is certainly true in North America where she had the biggest selling album in both the USA and Canada. There are, however, many other acts, both old and new, which are helping to maintain the UK's enviable export record.

Thirteen albums sold more than 1m copies in the USA in 2011, the same as in 2010. In both years these albums contributed 23.3m sales to the US album market, but in 2011 the best seller (Adele's *21*) sold 5.8m copies compared to 3.4m of Eminem's *Recovery* in 2010.

The success of Adele in 2011 has rightly generated enormous amounts of media coverage and her impact on the share of British music sales around the world is substantial.

Her achievements in the US were perhaps best summed up by the fact that she was presented with six Grammy awards in 2012, a total only ever bettered by three artists. She was also only the third artist ever to win the three key categories of Song, Record and Album of the Year in one evening.

Among the new artists making an impression in 2011 were Marsha Ambrosius (ex-Floetry), Jessie J and metal act Asking Alexandria, all of whom sold more than 100,000 albums last year.

WOMEN AGAIN LEAD THE WAY IN 2011

As in 2010, female artists were well represented among the best selling British artists in the US in 2011. Adele, Florence & The Machine, Susan Boyle and Amy Winehouse all had two titles among the best sellers and Marsha Ambrosius, Sade and Jessie J all made the UK top 20.

Florence & The Machine's success has been steadily building. Since its 2009 release, *Lungs* has sold a total of almost 900,000 copies and second album *Ceremonials* followed up convincingly with more than 400,000 sales since its October release, peaking at number six on the Billboard 200.

As usual there are many long-established artists among the best sellers such as The Beatles, Pink Floyd, Eric Clapton, Elton John and Led Zeppelin who have long been a bedrock of UK sales overseas, but there are always examples of newer acts that are beginning to make an impression in the American market.

In 2011 these included Two Door Cinema Club (83,000 sales) and The Joy Formidable, who sold 35,000 copies of their debut album *The Big Roar*.

UK Artists Share of Album Sales in USA & Canada

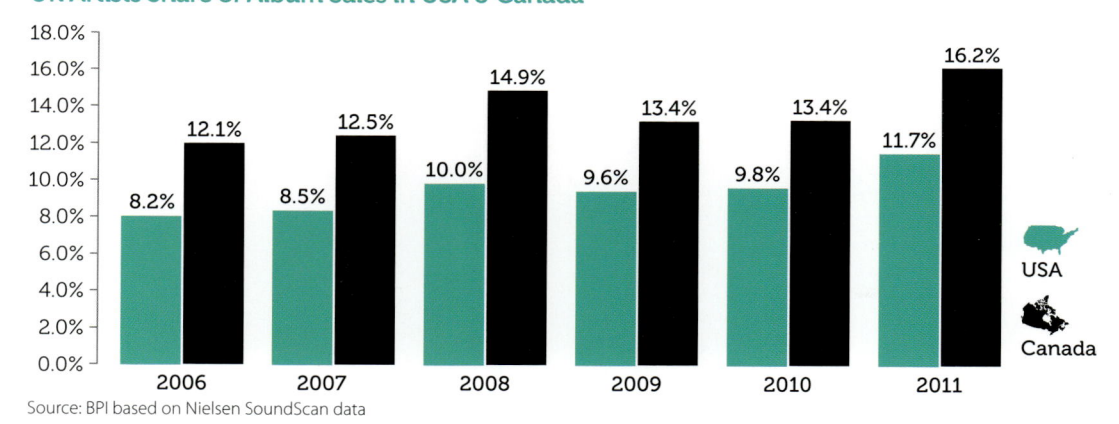

Year	USA	Canada
2006	8.2%	12.1%
2007	8.5%	12.5%
2008	10.0%	14.9%
2009	9.6%	13.4%
2010	9.8%	13.4%
2011	11.7%	16.2%

Source: BPI based on Nielsen SoundScan data

UK Artists Selling 1m+ Tracks in USA in 2011 (units m)

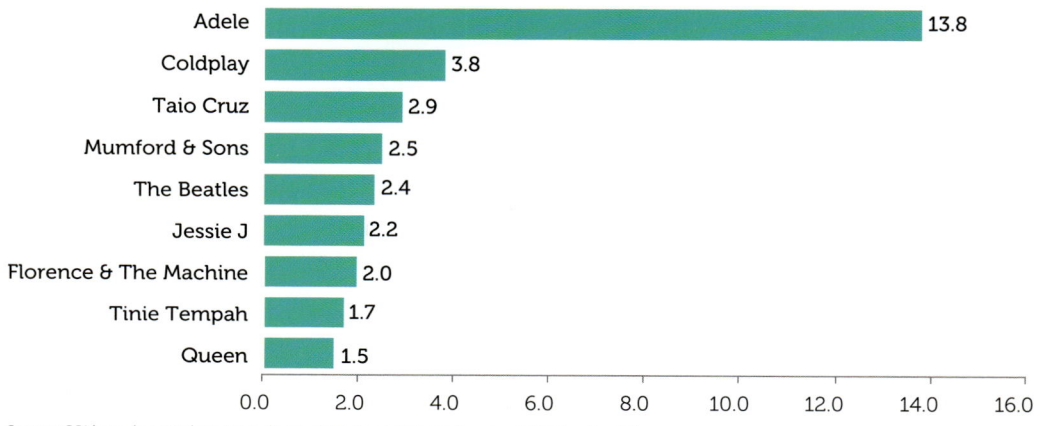

Artist	Units (m)
Adele	13.8
Coldplay	3.8
Taio Cruz	2.9
Mumford & Sons	2.5
The Beatles	2.4
Jessie J	2.2
Florence & The Machine	2.0
Tinie Tempah	1.7
Queen	1.5

Source: BPI based on Nielsen SoundScan data. Analysis based on top 3,000 tracks of the year

ADELE TRACK SALES APPROACH 14M IN 2011

In addition to selling 5.8m copies of **21** in the US in 2011, **Adele** also sold 13.8m single tracks. Using a ratio of 11 tracks per album, this represents the equivalent of an additional 1.25m album sales.

Other artists to pass the 1m sales mark included **Coldplay** with 3.8m sales (up from 1.5m in 2010), **Taio Cruz** (who has now sold more than 10m tracks in the past two years), **Mumford & Sons** and **The Beatles** whose track sales increased from 1.3m in 2010 to 2.4m, reflecting a full year's availability on iTunes. **Jessie J** and **Florence & The Machine** also enjoyed substantial success in 2011 with each selling more than 2m tracks for the first time.

There were 294 titles by UK artists in the top 3,000 single track downloads of the year, compared to 257 in 2010. Together they accounted for 8.6% of sales, up from 6.7%. This was the highest share of the singles market since 2008 when UK artists accounted for 9.8% of sales, driven by **Leona Lewis**, **MIA** and others.

Top 10 Albums by British Artists in USA 2011

	Overall	Artist	Title	Company
1	1	Adele	21	XL Recordings / Columbia
2	6	Mumford & Sons	Sigh No More	Glassnote
3	13	Coldplay	Mylo Xyloto	Capitol
4	17	Adele	19	XL Recordings / Columbia
5	46	Florence & The Machine	Lungs	Universal
6	53	Susan Boyle	Someone To Watch Over Me	Columbia
7	59	Florence & The Machine	Ceremonials	Universal
8	62	Marsha Ambrosius	Late Nights & Early Mornings	J Records
9	112	Radiohead	The King Of Limbs	TBD Records
10	115	The Beatles	1	Capitol

Source: BPI based on Nielsen SoundScan data

THE CANADIAN MARKET

IFPI data shows the Canadian market to be the seventh largest market in the world and chart analysis over the years has demonstrated its receptiveness to UK music, with British artists accounting for over 12% of album sales in each of the past five years.

Adele's *21* sold almost a million albums there in 2011, well over twice as many as the biggest seller of 2010, **Eminem**'s *Recovery*. It was also a good year for **Coldplay** and **Mumford & Sons**, who both made an appearance in the year-end Top 10. These successes – along with strong results for artists such as **Susan Boyle** and **Florence & The Machine** – helped the British share of the albums market up to 16.2%, by far the highest in recent years.

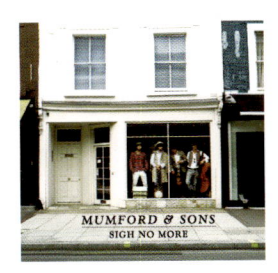

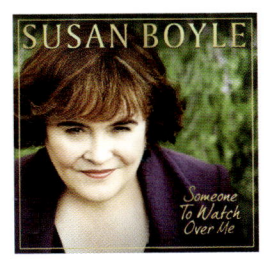

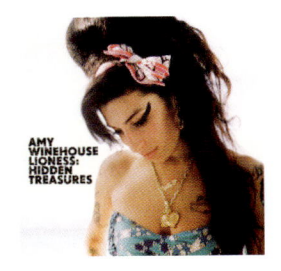

Top 10 Albums by British Artists in Canada 2011

	Overall	Artist	Title	Company
1	1	Adele	21	XL Recordings / Columbia
2	6	Coldplay	Mylo Xyloto	EMI
3	7	Mumford & Sons	Sigh No More	Glassnote
4	11	Adele	19	XL Recordings / Columbia
5	40	Susan Boyle	Someone To Watch Over Me	Sony Music
6	54	Amy Winehouse	Lioness: Hidden Treasures	Universal Island
7	56	Amy Winehouse	Back To Black	Universal Island
8	57	Florence & The Machine	Ceremonials	Universal
9	69	Florence & The Machine	Lungs	Universal
10	74	Johnny Reid	A Place Called Love	EMI

Source: BPI based on Nielsen SoundScan data

Picture Credits

Cover	Adele	*John Marshall/JMenternational.com*
Cover/14	Coldplay	*Sarah Lee*
Cover/16	Jessie J	*Tom van Schelven*
16	Noel Gallagher	*Lawrence Watson*
22	Professor Green	*Desmond Muckian*
34	Courtesy of HMV	
36	© Gallofilm – Fotolia.com	
38	Courtesy of HMV	
52	Caro Emerald	*Adrie Mouthaan*
55	Aloe Blacc	*Dan Monick*
57	Courtesy of Spotify	
58	Courtesy of Facebook	
59	Courtesy of HMV	
61	© RA2 Studio – Fotolia.com	
62	Courtesy of Nokia	
65	Courtesy of Napster	
68	Courtesy of HMV	